LET ME ASK YOU A QUESTION

CONVERSATIONS WITH JESUS

MATTHEW CROASMUN

UPPER ROOM BOOKS®
NASHVILLE

Cover design: Spencer Fuller, Faceout Studio
Typesetting and interior design: PerfecType, Nashville, TN

ISBN (print): 978-0-8358-1799-8
ISBN (mobi): 978-0-8358-1800-1
ISBN (epub): 978-0-8358-1801-8

Printed in the United States of America

CONTENTS

ACKNOWLEDGMENTS

The exercises in this book were first developed for use during the 2013 Lenten season at the Elm City Vineyard Church. To my beloved church home, it is a joy and a privilege to follow Jesus with you! A few chapters were originally sermons I preached during that Lenten season; others preached sermons during that series whose ideas, no doubt, contributed to the relevant chapters in this book for which I am grateful: Sidney Noland, Robb Evans, and Josh Williams. The whole undertaking—the theme for both the sermon series and the exercises—was the brainchild of my dear friend and colleague in ministry, Todd Kennedy. Chapters for sermons I didn't originally preach in 2013 were helped tremendously through the opportunity to preach a mini-series on these texts at the Shoreline Vineyard Church in the summer of 2017. That summer, I was aided immensely by the diligent work of Nathan Jowers, whose studious editorial eye helped both in the preparation of those sermons and with the transition from sermon manuscripts to book chapters. I could not have asked for a better research assistant. Many people—Jesus-followers and truth-seekers alike—at the Elm City Vineyard, Shoreline Vineyard, and beyond have used these exercises and given me extraordinarily valuable feedback as to how to refine them. I should also acknowledge my students at Yale. I didn't expect to refer so often to the Life Worth Living course as I wrote this book, but that class has become a tremendously fruitful space for me both intellectually and personally. Thanks go especially to those who gave me permission to share some of their experiences from which I have learned so much. And, of course, my family, Hannah and Junia, have contributed so much to the production of this book, most of all through their patience with a husband and father so often preaching and writing on weekends and in the evenings long after the workday should be over. I thank God for you most of all.

"I will also ask you a question."
—Jesus (Luke 20:3)

AN INVITATION

Often, people think of Jesus as the man with all the answers. Some people love that about him, while it has made others keep their distance. But, again and again in the Bible (more than 300 times, according to my colleague Martin Copenhaver), Jesus asks questions. He engages people—his followers, his critics, and strangers he meets along the way—inviting responses from them, genuinely interested in what they have to say. This book invites you into the same kind of conversations with Jesus. It will lead you into these stories from long ago so that you may encounter Jesus in the questions he asks.

To do so, you must read these stories as more than ancient history. Not that there isn't value in reading the Bible with its ancient setting in mind; as a Bible scholar, much of what I do professionally includes reading these stories in the context of their historical environment. But history is by no means the most important aspect of the Bible—certainly not for me. What keeps me coming back to these stories are my experiences with a living presence I've encountered in them: the presence of Jesus. And that's what I want for you as well: an encounter with Jesus. Whether you've come to this book full of faith, full of questions, or both; whether you've come with some assurance that you know who Jesus is or you aren't sure what to think about God, faith, or Jesus—I hope you will find yourself in conversation with Jesus. My desire is that you'll know these sorts of conversations are real because you've experienced them for yourself.

So let me encourage you. If this whole encountering Jesus thing sounds crazy, consider the exercises in this book an experiment, an opportunity to see if Jesus is real and alive. Try them out and see whether Jesus meets you in his questions. See whether you find yourself entering into a dynamic back-and-forth with the living Christ. If not, my sense is that you'll have lost relatively little for taking the risk to try it out. But if you do—if today or tomorrow or next week or next month you find that Jesus is real, alive, and at work in your world—that's worth taking some risk, right?

. . . . . .

Over the course of this book, you will use Jesus' questions as recorded in the Bible as entry points for your own conversations with him. Each chapter contains a short reflection on one of Jesus' questions and five exercises. I present these exercises as *daily* activities. If that works for you, great. In my experience, some need more time to give these questions a chance to "breathe." I've had friends engage with this material over six months rather than six weeks, and it allowed them to sit with Jesus and process what he was saying to them at the pace they found most helpful. Feel free to move at whatever pace works for you. The chapters essentially serve as extended invitations to engage with Jesus through the exercises that follow, woven together with notes from my own experience dialoguing with Jesus. Fundamentally, I hope your time will be spent engaging not with those notes and invitations but with the exercises themselves. Reading this book without engaging in the mode of prayer it commends would be like reading a cookbook without ever trying one of the recipes or techniques.

The format of the exercises is simple: First, you'll see a passage from the Bible, including a question Jesus asks in bold. A short reflection follows the Bible passage, designed to help you engage with Jesus' question as he asked it in the Gospels and as he is asking it of you right now. The facing page holds an opportunity to "continue the conversation" with Jesus, beginning with the question he asks in the Bible passage. This page is laid out as a dialogue in a play with Jesus' words and space for you to write a response. The goal is to engage in a dialogue so that as you respond, you can sense how Jesus might be further responding to you. You may find it helpful or even necessary to continue writing what you hear Jesus saying, capturing your sense of his side of the conversation as you go. If this practice is new, it may seem odd at first, but this type of conversational prayer journaling has been part of Christian traditions for centuries.

· · · · · ·

There's an old joke that says when we tell people we talk to God, they think we're pious; when we tell them God talks back, they think we're crazy. Indeed, if we're not used to thinking about prayer as a *conversation*, it can seem scary or even impious to dare think we've heard Jesus' voice, much less dare to write down what we think we've heard. But, as the Bible tells us, conversing with God has been part of the human experience from the very beginning. In Genesis, the first words uttered to the human creature were the words of our Maker. And after naming the animals, the first words addressed by the human *to* anyone were addressed to God. Perhaps that first conversation didn't end on the best terms, but later conversations with God weren't always full of easy cordiality either. God's particular people, Israel, receive their name from a man (originally named Jacob) who contends and wrestles with God. Moses, the great liberator of the people of God, converses with God and, at times, pleads with God on behalf of the Israelites. The Psalms attributed to David, the great king, which give voice to the full range of human emotion, are all addressed to God.

By the time Jesus arrives on the scene, his invitation to conversation is not exactly a radical innovation but a continuation of the traditions of God's people. The church, in different ways and in different eras, has adopted structures for facilitating this conversation and drawing us back to it. Almost five hundred years ago, Ignatius of Loyola, founder of the Jesuits, recommended regular, honest conversation with God—a practice named *colloquy*—at the conclusion of a time of meditation on scripture. These days, Christians from many traditions engage in "listening prayer," "conversational prayer," or "dialogical prayer." As they do so, they are surrounded by a great cloud of witnesses. The experiment we're about to undertake aims at this ancient mystery. If we *do* sense a voice speaking back to us, addressing us in these questions, we've found more than a new personal spiritual practice; we've stumbled into the way of life of the people of God from around the world and across millennia.

· · · · · ·

Our goal in this experiment of responding to Jesus' questions is to engage relationally. The goal is *not* to seek the "right" answers. In many cases, this will be obvious enough; there won't be one "right" answer. In other cases, we may be tempted to think that a "right" answer exists (indeed, in some cases, the context of a passage itself provides such an answer). But even if and when the passage itself supplies a "right" answer, answering honestly better serves to build the relationship we're after—even if that honest answer is the "wrong" one. Time and again in the Gospels, "right" answers serve people poorly, and "wrong" answers lead to profound encounters with Jesus. Engaging honestly with Jesus always moves people toward a closer relationship with him. My hunch is that the same will be true of our encounter with Jesus through the questions he asks us in these pages.

Some of the questions Jesus asks cut right to the heart of difficulties in our lives. If we decide to let Jesus ask his questions and we resolve to answer them honestly, we'll be confronted with some ugly truths in our hearts and lives we'd rather not deal with. This is to be expected; any good relationship helps us know ourselves better—including seeing our faults more clearly. When this happens, we must remember to distinguish between the experiences of *conviction* and *condemnation*. Though both come from encountering ugly truths about ourselves, conviction often comes from God, but condemnation never comes from God. Condemnation is conviction robbed of hope. Condemnation says, "You're ugly, you're broken, and you're never going to change." Conviction says, "There may be ugliness, there may be brokenness, but that's not who you *are*. Who you are—God's beloved creation—is beautiful and whole. By God's grace, you can be—and indeed you are becoming—this truest self." When these questions become difficult, we can remember that while Jesus will convict us of sin (things that work against our flourishing and the flourishing of the world), he will never condemn us. And when he does convict us, he does so in order to draw us toward transformation into his likeness.

Finally, as we listen for the voice of Jesus in these questions and the conversations that come from them, the presence of others can be vital in helping us discern what we hear. Learning to hear the voice of God is no easy thing, and we need support along the way. The people of God have always had processes for discerning in community. This communal discernment is at the core of how Paul, the ancient church planter, describes the church. As a discerning community, the church has access to the mind of Christ, and members can work together to weigh the significance of what they hear Jesus saying to them. So as we engage in this experiment, let's invite others to join us and help us process what we hear and what we might do as a result. Let's now turn our attention to the questions Jesus asks.

Week 1

What Do You Want Me to Do for You?

When I was younger, music was the center of my world. I played the piano, saxophone, and guitar, but, more than anything else, I had a passion for writing music. My high school had a pretty great music department with lots of opportunities to learn and grow as a musician. I really connected with the teachers, save for one: Dr. Lambert. I didn't dislike him so much as I feared him. Everyone did. He was the chair of the department. It wasn't only the students who feared him; the faculty did as well, which only compounded the students' sense that he was someone we oughtn't trifle with. Needless to say, when Dr. Lambert called me out of band rehearsal one morning to meet in his office, I was worried. I slunk into the room, bracing for the worst. He asked me to sit down. He sort of looked me over, sizing me up, and then he asked, "If you had one less class to take this semester and could spend that hour doing anything you wanted, what would you do?"

I was shocked. I'm pretty sure I just stammered something like, "I'm sorry?" So he repeated his question, and finally I answered, "Well, shoot, I don't know. I suppose I'd spend my time writing and recording music."

"Alright," Dr. Lambert replied. "Every day after lunch, I want you here in the department, writing something, recording something, creating something. We'll write it up as an independent study. If you want to learn some music theory, we can do that. If you want to take an AP exam or two at the end, we can do that too."

Needless to say, that was the best "class" I ever took. It changed my life. During that hour every day, I wrote the music that formed the core of my college applications and put me on the track I ran on for the next five years of my life.

· · · · · ·

We begin with a similar, shockingly generous question that Jesus asks: "What do you want me to do for you?" This question shows up twice in the span of just a few verses at the end of the tenth chapter of Mark, the oldest of the accounts of Jesus' life. The repetition of this single question in the last two passages in this chapter suggests that both these stories are about *desire*. They're about what we want, what's worth wanting, and where we ought to turn to get it.

Let's start with the second of these two stories. As Jesus and his disciples—his closest friends and followers—are traveling together, they encounter a very persistent man who wants Jesus' attention.

> As Jesus and his disciples, together with a large crowd, were leaving [Jericho], a blind man, Bartimaeus (which means "son of Timaeus"), was sitting by the roadside begging. When he heard that it was Jesus of Nazareth, he began to shout, "Jesus, Son of David, have mercy on me!" Many rebuked him and told him to be quiet, but he shouted all the more, "Son of David, have mercy on me!" Jesus stopped and said, "Call him." So they called to the blind man, "Cheer up! On your feet! He's calling you." Throwing his cloak side, he jumped to his feet and came to Jesus. "What do you want me to do for you?" Jesus asked him. The blind man said, "Rabbi, I want to see." "Go," said Jesus, "your faith has healed you." Immediately he received his sight and followed Jesus along the road. (Mark 10:46-52)

Bartimaeus sits beside the road, begging. He's looking for money. As Bartimaeus calls out for Jesus' attention, he essentially is repeating what he has been shouting all day—"Have mercy on me!"—but adding Jesus' name, personalizing his panhandling. Yet, to the surprise of many, it *works*. Jesus stops and asks someone to bring Bartimaeus to him. And then he asks him the question I want to focus on: "What do you want me to do for you?" It's a reasonable question, and Bartimaeus has a real decision to make. Does he ask for money—which is what he's been asking for all day—or does he ask for what he really wants, what he really *needs*? Bartimaeus goes for broke, and he walks away healed—actually, he doesn't just walk away, he follows Jesus. His life's orientation changes forever.

But wait a minute. Jesus' question is shocking. Isn't this the opposite of how God works? Powerful people aren't supposed to ask what they can do for us; powerful people tell us what we need to do for them. And God is *very* powerful, so we may be inclined to think that God would be just as demanding—or even more so. But people who have experienced God throughout the ages have remarked again and again on this surprising fact. Isaiah, the ancient prophet, remarks, "Since ancient times no one has heard, no ear has perceived, no eye has seen any God besides you, who acts on behalf of those who wait for him" (64:4). God also makes this point in Psalm 50:

> I bring no charges against you concerning your sacrifices
> or concerning your burnt offerings, which are ever before me.
> I have no need of a bull from your stall
> or of goats from your pens,
> for every animal of the forest is mine,
> and the cattle on a thousand hills.
> I know every bird in the mountains,
> and the insects in the fields are mine.
> If I were hungry I would not tell you,
> for the world is mine, and all that is in it. (vv. 8-12)

If we caught some sarcasm there, we're not imagining it. But God's point, as I understand it, is plain enough: If God ever had a need (which seems unlikely), we're not exactly God's go-to source. Our relationship with God isn't founded on us providing God what God needs; it's founded on God providing us what we need. That's just how it works between an all-powerful God and only somewhat-powerful people.

Ultimately, Jesus' question to Bartimaeus reveals a similar profound truth about the character of God. Again, in Mark 10, Jesus makes this clear to his disciples who are confused on this point: "Even the Son of Man did not come to be served, but to serve, and to give his life as a ransom for many" (v. 45). Jesus came to serve, not to be served. Maybe that takes our view of God and turns it on its head, but there it is: God's angle isn't what God can get out of us or what God can get us to do for God. No, what drives God into relationship with people isn't what God can get out of them but what God can do for them. And this frame of mind drives Jesus into conversation with Bartimaeus. Bartimaeus cries out, "Have mercy on me!" and Jesus is moved by compassion to ask Bartimaeus a question, to write him a divine blank check: "What do you want me to do for you?"

Bartimaeus answers plainly enough: "Rabbi, I want to see."

"Your faith has healed you," Jesus replies.

Bartimaeus is healed. It is his *faith* that has healed him. *But what faith?* we may wonder. *What has Bartimaeus done? How has he exhibited his faith? All he did was sit by the side of the road and beg for Jesus to help him.* Apparently, these actions themselves express a sort of faith—faith enough to heal a blind man. In other words, trusting Jesus with our desires is itself an act of faith. Trusting Jesus with our desires requires that we at least entertain the possibility that Jesus has the power to do what we ask. Opening ourselves to the idea that Jesus is alive, has God's ear, and is in the business of responding to people when they cry out for help is an act of faith—and no small act at that. It requires risk, but risk and faith often go hand in hand.

· · · · · ·

A few years ago, my wife, Hannah, and I were trying to buy a house, and we faced myriad challenges along the way: problems with the mortgage, problems with the inspection, problems with the sellers. Throughout the process, I remember editing my prayers, trying to make sure I kept my requests reasonable. I prayed for God's help with particular problems, but asking for what I really wanted—that we would get the house—seemed too risky. It somehow felt crass. So I prayed instead for God's will to be done or something pious like that, feigning a disinterest in the outcome. In part, I was doing my best to protect God's honor, making sure that my "faith"—my theological system—had a way out if, in fact, God didn't come through. It was theological bet-hedging, a painful sort of spiritual gymnastics that included redacting my prayers so that, no matter what happened, I could confidently count them as answered in the affirmative.

Finally, I felt Jesus speak to me, asking, "What do you want?" Not "What do you think I want for you?" or "What do you think you *should* ask for?" But rather, "What do *you* want?" I didn't take this as a guarantee that I would get whatever I asked; rather, it was an invitation to take a leap of faith, to trust Jesus with my desires—win or lose. That's the key, really. We bring our honest desires before Jesus not because we're guaranteed to get what we ask for but because if and when we *are* disappointed, we're better off being disappointed in dialogue with Jesus than on our own. Jesus invited me to be candid in my prayers in part because if things *didn't* work out, I'd be in a better place of honesty to process my disappointment. If I self-edited my prayers, my desires—and, potentially, my disappointments—would remain my own. But if I brought it all before Jesus in childlike honesty, any prospective disappointment would benefit from the intimacy that honesty had established.

I remember the tremendous release and freedom I felt in finally praying honestly, saying, *I don't know what you want or what I should want. I just know that I'd really like to have this house. If Hannah and I could buy it and live in it—that's what I want. Can you do that?* And at that moment, a huge burden fell from my shoulders. And, indeed, later that fall, we moved into our house.

That moment of honesty has changed the way I view the house. It's not my house; it's God's house. Hannah and I received it as a gift from God. We enjoy it and we do our best to use it for God's good purposes—to bless others. That house has sheltered those who had nowhere else to go. It has been home base for our church—the closest our church has had to permanent physical space since we don't own a building. And when I think about all the things God has done in that house—the lives God has touched, the community God has built—it's clear that the house has been a gift.

So let's consider these questions: What if Jesus is alive and at work in the world? What if Jesus is at work for our good? If Jesus were asking us the question he asks Bartimaeus right now, what would we ask for? How would we respond? Could we dare to take his question seriously and answer honestly? These follow-up questions are important, especially if we've been following Jesus for a while and have begun to forget who is asking us the question in the first place. Jesus gives us the possibility of restored sight, but perhaps we've been asking for spare change instead of life-changing transformation.

· · · · · ·

At this point, I imagine that many readers are thinking, *This is great and all, but is Jesus really just about meeting our needs? Does he just do whatever we ask him to do? Is Jesus the vending machine God? Should we imagine Jesus as a genie in a bottle? We just ask for whatever we want, and he gives it to us.* I don't think so. And, interestingly enough, the story right before this in Mark 10 speaks to exactly this issue:

> James and John, the sons of Zebedee, came to [Jesus]. "Teacher," they said, "we want you to do for us whatever we ask." "What do you want me to do for you?" he asked. They replied, "Let one of us sit at your right and the other at your left in your glory." "You don't know what you are asking," Jesus said. "Can you drink the cup I drink or be baptized with the baptism I am baptized with?" "We can," they answered. Jesus said to them, "You will drink the cup I drink and be baptized with the baptism I am baptized with, but to sit at my right

or left is not for me to grant. Those places belong to those for whom
they have been prepared." (vv. 35-40)

James and John are like political advisors at the end of a presidential cam-
paign, starting to angle for cabinet appointments in the coming administration.
It's clear from the beginning of the encounter that they are trying to manipulate
Jesus. Their ploy is almost laughably childish: They want a promise of a posi-
tive answer before they ask their question. Jesus won't be duped. He refuses to
answer without knowing what they want. "What do you want me to do for
you?" he asks, using the same question he'll ask Bartimaeus later.

James and John come clean: They want the two top positions in Jesus' kingdom. When Jesus has "made" it, they want to be at his right and at his left. "You
don't know what you are asking," Jesus says. And it's true—they don't. As Jesus
indicates at the end of the passage, they fundamentally have misunderstood *what*
Jesus' glory is all about and *when* Jesus will enter his glory.

Jesus' glory is not like a cheesy sports movie. Jesus isn't striving for success
in the way James and John imagine. Rather, the positions on Jesus' right and
left that James and John have requested are spoken for, as Jesus says. The next
time Mark talks about "right and left," he describes two criminals crucified with
Jesus—"one on his right and one on his left" (Mark 15:27)—revealing, most sur-
prisingly of all, that somehow, in Jesus' upside-down world, Jesus is in his *glory*
on the cross. Jesus redefines greatness for his followers: Greatness isn't about
puffing ourselves up or using our power and authority to maintain a position;
greatness is about service. The life of the One who came to serve rather than to
be served reaches its apex when he lays down his life for the sake of many. Suffice
it to say, this is not the sort of greatness that James and John are after. And so, in
part, Jesus protects them when he responds to their request to share in his glory
with an abrupt, "You don't know what you are asking."

But I think there's more to it than just that. Jesus is also saying, "I know
you're wanting greatness. That's not a bad thing. But you don't know what real
greatness looks like. You don't know what real greatness costs. Have you considered what it is you're asking for? Ultimately, I think you're *right* to ask for it.

You're right to desire *true* greatness. But you would feel confused, disappointed, or, frankly, cheated if I offered you my sort of greatness. If I give you what you're asking, you'll receive the places of honor at my right and left when I'm on the cross. That's real glory, but I'm not sure you'd thank me for giving it to you. Your sense of what you want—even more, of what's *worth wanting*—needs revision." One day, Jesus explains, they will follow in his footsteps in a life of self-sacrifice; they will be *great* in the economy of God. But for the time being, James and John need to think deeply about their answer to Jesus' question.

Ultimately, Jesus wants James and John to reconsider and refine their answer to his question: "What do you *really* want me to do for you? Do you *really* want the cheap sort of glory you're asking for when I'm about to turn the world upside-down and show that true authority comes through service and true power through weakness? Do you *really* just want political spoils when, by laying down your life, you could be a part of the coming revolution that will change the world forever? Why would you settle for so little? Why set your sights so low?" In asking for political power and glory, James and John make the mistake Bartimaeus avoids. They ask for pocket change instead of restored sight.

I wonder if the same isn't true of us. We think Jesus is putting us off because we've asked for too much, for something too difficult, or for something too extravagant. Instead, Jesus looks at our request, considers our answer to his question, and asks, "Why so little? Why are you so desperate for money and jobs and prestige and financial security and success? Why do you aim so low? Why not ask me for true riches? Why not ask for purpose much deeper than a job? for glory that looks like service? for abiding security within that allows you to take risks with your life? for a life of obedience that rescues you from the fear of failure?"

Jesus wants an opportunity to redefine for us what is *worth wanting*. Jesus isn't about offering us whatever we want. He loves us too much for that. Jesus wants to give us what has true worth, but our standards for worth, in many respects, are skewed. As we wrestle with Jesus about our desires—and I do believe that the first step is to be honest about what we want, right or wrong—we need to give him permission to do some reconfiguring at that most fundamental level by defining what is worth wanting. Only then are our lives built on a firm foundation. Only then can we live with the expectation that we won't get to the end of our lives and find that what we wanted wasn't worth wanting in the first place. Amid our skewed sense of what has the most value in the world, Jesus looks at us with compassion and asks, "Why do you ask for so little when I'm offering so much? What do you *really* want me to do for you? What is truly worth wanting?"

· · · · · ·

This final question—"What is truly worth wanting?"—is one I've been wrestling with for a long time. Along the way, I've realized that what we want isn't a set of discrete things or outcomes or feelings or even character traits. We want something more holistic than that. What drives us is an entire vision of a good life. Somewhere, deep down, we have a vision of the life that we want for ourselves, for our communities, and for our children or those who come after us. That life isn't hardly a "thing" at all, nor is it something we can possess. Once we realize that what's worth wanting is a *life* of a certain sort, we begin asking a new question: "What is a life worth living?"

Each year, I have the privilege of teaching a class titled "Life Worth Living," and I embark on a journey with Yale undergraduates to explore life's most important question in light of many the world's religious and philosophical traditions. In the course, as we hear from these different traditions, we also hear from one another by asking ourselves, *What do we think makes a life most worth living?* While there are lots of different answers to the question, for many of my students, it comes down to this: The purpose of life is to make an impact, to change the world, to do something great—maybe even *be* someone great. Not unlike James and John, *greatness* is their goal.

I can relate to that. I've always wanted to be great. When I first came to college in my students' shoes, I was driven by this dream of greatness—the sideways fruit of Dr. Lambert's generous offer. Coming out of high school, I wanted to be a composer and a conductor of a major symphony orchestra. I was going to be great—or at least famous. Often, I couldn't tell the difference. But if I ever could pull the two apart, it was unsettling to imagine that greatness might come without fame. I wasn't sure I *wanted* greatness without fame or widespread recognition. My four years of college were in large part about God pulling apart this twisted desire for "greatness" from God's offer of *true* greatness. It took years to try to find what was worth wanting in the mess of what I wanted so badly. Eventually, I concluded that what I wanted out of music wasn't worth wanting; the life I imagined with music its center simply wasn't the one most worth living.

Coming to know myself instead as a teacher has shifted the way I think about "greatness" in my life. As a teacher, "greatness" is all about *legacy*. Great teachers tend not to arrive at places of great influence or tremendous accolade. Great teachers become footnotes to the stories of the lives of their students—or of their students' students. As a teacher, it is quite likely that I will be off-camera during the most important moments in my life's story, moments when perhaps my name is forgotten but God's name is glorified. As I begin to think this way, the anxiety of "greatness" begins to melt away—not replaced by lowered expectations or settling for mediocrity but expanded into the story of God and God's people. Twenty years later, when I look around the seminar table at my students, it strikes me: I wouldn't even have known to *ask* for this. But this, it seems, is what is worth wanting.

· · · · · ·

Throughout this chapter, as we've unpacked Jesus' question, we've found two significant questions embedded within it. First, what do we want Jesus to do for us? Remember, Jesus said that Bartimaeus's honest answer to this question was a substantial step of faith. Our first task is to ask and answer the question without trying to make ourselves sound pious, without trying to give the "right" answer. Instead, we can be honest about our real needs and desires.

Second, what is *worth wanting*? Both stories we looked at have this moment of clarification. Bartimaeus has to choose: Should he merely ask Jesus for money, or should he ask for what he really wants and needs? At the end of James's and John's story, they find themselves in that process of clarification, wondering what true greatness is and what they want, wondering how their desires are going to be transformed in the process of taking them to Jesus. This clarification process is important for us as well.

God is a giver of good gifts, and Jesus invites us to engage with him in precisely that way, as he asks us, in all earnestness, "What do you want me to do for you?" If we answer honestly, I have no doubt that Jesus will meet us in the conversation that ensues, sometimes giving us exactly what we want, other times meeting us in our disappointment, and always helping refine what is genuinely worth wanting.

Monday, Week 1

· · · · · · · · · · · ·

Read Mark 10:46-52.

As Jesus and his disciples, together with a large crowd, were leaving [Jericho], a blind man, Bartimaeus (which means "son of Timaeus"), was sitting by the roadside begging. When he heard that it was Jesus of Nazareth, he began to shout, "Jesus, Son of David, have mercy on me!" Many rebuked him and told him to be quiet, but he shouted all the more, "Son of David, have mercy on me!" Jesus stopped and said, "Call him." So they called to the blind man, "Cheer up! On your feet! He's calling you." Throwing his cloak aside, he jumped to his feet and came to Jesus. "**What do you want me to do for you?**" Jesus asked him. The blind man said, "Rabbi, I want to see." "Go," said Jesus, "your faith has healed you." Immediately he received his sight and followed Jesus along the road.

Reflection

It seems almost too good to be true. The famous Jesus not only stops and addresses Bartimaeus but also offers him a blank check: "What do you want me to do for you?" Could it possibly be this simple? Jesus' question reveals one of the most striking things about his character: He has come not to be served but to serve. Bartimaeus responds honestly and with real need—"Rabbi, I want to see"—and Jesus responds with compassion, healing Bartimaeus and adding a new follower to his community. Jesus is interested in the deep desires of our heart. He won't always give us what we ask for, but he is interested in what we want. He invites us to come to him for those things. Let's bring these deep desires of our heart to Jesus, trust him with them, and see what will happen when we answer his question honestly.

Continue the Conversation

Jesus: What do you want me to do for you?

Me: ....

....

....

....

....

....

....

....

....

....

....

....

....

Tuesday, Week 1

· · · · · · · · · · · ·

Read Mark 10:35-45.

James and John, the sons of Zebedee, came to him. "Teacher," they said, "we want you to do for us whatever we ask." **"What do you want me to do for you?"** he asked. They replied, "Let one of us sit at your right and the other at your left in your glory." "You don't know what you are asking," Jesus said. "Can you drink the cup I drink or be baptized with the baptism I am baptized with?" "We can," they answered. Jesus said to them, "You will drink the cup I drink and be baptized with the baptism I am baptized with, but to sit at my right or left is not for me to grant. These places belong to those for whom they have been prepared." When the ten heard about this, they became indignant with James and John. Jesus called them together and said, "You know that those who are regarded as rulers of the Gentiles lord it over them, and their high officials exercise authority over them. Not so with you. Instead, whoever wants to become great among you must be your servant, and whoever wants to be first must be slave of all. For even the Son of Man did not come to be served, but to serve, and to give his life as a ransom for many."

Reflection

James and John are the other side of the same coin as Bartimaeus. They want Jesus to give them an answer before they've even asked their question. They want him to commit to doing whatever they want without engaging him in relationship. Jesus doesn't bite; he makes no promises. Nevertheless, he asks them the same question he later asks Bartimaeus: "What do you want me to do for you?" James and John are looking for what they call "glory." They're looking for prestige, power, and reputation—quite a different definition from how Jesus sees *glory*. Two things seem to bother Jesus: (1) Jesus knows that feeding James's and John's desire for these things won't actually help them at all. Jesus only gives good gifts, and this would be a bad one. (2) Jesus knows they're barking up the wrong tree. If they want prestige, Jesus' "glory" is hardly the place they're going to find it. Later, in Mark 15:27, we see that the people on Jesus' right and left are the two criminals crucified with him, proclaiming to us that Jesus is in his glory on the cross. This, presumably, is not what James and John are looking for. So Jesus replies with some clarifying questions about what James and John really want. He turns their attention from what they *want* to what's *worth wanting*. How might Jesus do this for us as well?

Continue the Conversation

Jesus: What do you want me to do for you?

Me: ....

....

....

....

....

....

....

....

....

....

....

....

....

....

Wednesday, Week 1

. . . .

Read John 1:35-39, NRSV.

The next day John again was standing with two of his disciples, and as he watched Jesus walk by, he exclaimed, "Look, here is the Lamb of God!" The two disciples heard him say this, and they followed Jesus. When Jesus turned and saw them following, he said to them, **"What are you looking for?"** They said to him, "Rabbi" (which translated means Teacher), "where are you staying?" He said to them, "Come and see." They came and saw where he was staying, and they remained with him that day.

Reflection

These two disciples of John the Baptist have reason to believe that there's something in Jesus worth pursuing. When they start following him, Jesus turns around and asks them, "What are you looking for?" This is another wide-open question that Jesus asks in order to reveal the hearts of his would-be followers. Their answer is deeper than we might notice. They ask Jesus, "Where are you staying?" The Greek word the disciples use translates to "abide" later in John's Gospel. Jesus says that "abiding" is key to understanding who he is and what kind of relationship he's looking for with us. Jesus wants to abide with God—that is, to rest in his relationship with God. In turn, he desires that we abide or rest in him so that we can live powerful, purposeful, and peaceful lives. So these disciples' response is better than perhaps they even know. They ask, "Where are you abiding?" or "What is the source of your life?" Ultimately, our deepest longing is to know Jesus and to understand his life-giving qualities, and responding to Jesus' question will help us take the next step in building a relationship with him.

Continue the Conversation

Jesus: What are you looking for?

Me: ....

....

....

....

....

....

....

....

....

....

....

....

....

Thursday, Week 1

· · · · · · · · · · · ·

Read John 5:1-9.

Jesus went up to Jerusalem for one of the Jewish festivals. Now there is in Jerusalem near the Sheep Gate a pool, which in Aramaic is called Bethesda and which is surrounded by five covered colonnades. Here a great number of disabled people used to lie—the blind, the lame, the paralyzed. One who was there had been an invalid for thirty-eight years. When Jesus saw him lying there and learned that he had been in this condition for a long time, he asked him, **"Do you want to get well?"** "Sir," the invalid replied, "I have no one to help me into the pool when the water is stirred. While I am trying to get in, someone else goes down ahead of me." Then Jesus said to him, "Get up! Pick up your mat and walk." At once the man was cured; he picked up his mat and walked.

Reflection

Jesus asks if the man wants to be healed, and the man answers with an explanation of why he can't be healed. Though Jesus' question seems to have an obvious answer, the question—"Do you want to get well?"—is worth asking. Often, when Jesus asks us this question, we offer excuses as to why change isn't possible. Instead of putting our faith and hope in Jesus, we place them in something else, something that inevitably falls short of providing what we need. Even so, Jesus knows we want to get well, and he offers healing.

Continue the Conversation

Jesus: Do you want to get well?

Me: I do sometimes put my hope in something else, I spend time enjoying other things but ultimatly I return to Jesus as my hope faith, because He reminds me where I should be.

I do need to have regular church attendance and reminders to read my Bible. I also need to be in Sunday School.

Friday, Week 1

. . . .

Read Luke 10:25-37.

On one occasion an expert in the law stood up to test Jesus. "Teacher," he asked, "what must I do to inherit eternal life?" "What is written in the Law?" he replied. **"How do you read it?"** He answered, " 'Love the Lord your God with all your heart and with all your soul and with all your strength and with all your mind'; and, 'Love your neighbor as yourself.' " "You have answered correctly," Jesus replied. "Do this and you will live." But he wanted to justify himself, so he asked Jesus, "And who is my neighbor?" In reply Jesus said: "A man was going down from Jerusalem to Jericho, when he was attacked by robbers. They stripped him of his clothes, beat him and went away, leaving him half dead. A priest happened to be going down the same road, and when he saw the man, he passed by on the other side. So too, a Levite, when he came to the place and saw him, passed by on the other side. But a Samaritan, as he traveled, came where the man was; and when he saw him, he took pity on him. He went to him and bandaged his wounds, pouring on oil and wine. Then he put the man on his own donkey, brought him to an inn and took care of him. The next day he took out two denarii and gave them to the innkeeper. 'Look after him,' he said, 'and when I return, I will reimburse you for any extra expense you may have.' Which of these three do you think was a neighbor to the man who fell into the hands of robbers?" The expert in the law replied, "The one who had mercy on him." Jesus told him, "Go and do likewise."

Reflection

A religious scholar has a religious question, but rather than answer him directly, Jesus asks him a question first: "What is written in the Law? How do you read it?" The question elicits further conversation, giving us one of the most memorable stories Jesus ever tells. As we engage with Jesus through his words in the Bible, we should remember that Jesus wants to know how scripture strikes us. He's not interested in the "right" answer—even when the scholar gives the "right" answer, Jesus addresses a deeper issue. Jesus wants to know what the text awakens in us, what response it elicits from us. So let's take a look at this passage again or at another biblical passage. Answer Jesus' question: "How do you read it?" Jesus wants to know what the Bible means to us so he can meet us in it.

Continue the Conversation

Jesus: How do you read it?

Me: _I should be taking care of those who can't care for themselves. We should also be helping those who have lost their way in this world._

Week 2

Has No One Condemned You?

I have the best job in the world. That's a bold statement to make, but I believe it's true. Along with my colleagues at the Yale Center for Faith & Culture, I spend my days writing and teaching about life's biggest questions. As I mentioned in the previous chapter, teaching is my particular passion, and I feel extraordinarily privileged to live out my calling by helping college students discern what makes life most worth living.

A while back, a friend informed me that a professor at another institution was mocking us on social media—specifically, calling my course frivolous, criticizing the university for teaching privileged students, and berating my colleagues and me for thinking we had something to offer when it came to wrestling with life's biggest questions. This professor was someone whose work I respected and, frankly, whose critiques I felt deeply. I love my job and am incredibly grateful for the opportunity to do what I do, but *of course* I struggle with the irony of talking about meaning and purpose—all of which point beyond oneself and one's privilege—in a context as elite and often self-centered as an Ivy League university. I tried to play it cool on the outside, but internally I was frantic.

As I obsessed about how to respond, trying to figure out what this person wanted me to do, I realized this: There's nothing for me to do. That wasn't the point of the comment. It wasn't made in an effort to help me or even to persuade me to pursue a different course of action. It was an opportunity to use my colleagues' and my work as an occasion for ridicule. It was an opportunity to *condemn* me and my work, to reject it out of hand.

Increasingly, condemnation is a hallmark of our society—particularly when it comes to social media. There is a reason, after all, that Jimmy Kimmel's "Mean Tweets" segment is so popular. But it goes deeper than mere personal slights. Our greatest cultural divides exhibit this dynamic. One group condemns another as lazy, irrational, unnatural, and un-American. The other group returns the favor, describing the first as racist, xenophobic, homophobic, and sexist. Condemnation is the medium through which our cultural divisions are realized, policed, and reinforced.

Condemnation is not a new social strategy. Jesus encountered his fair share as well. We find one such encounter in John 8:

> At dawn [Jesus] appeared again in the temple courts, where all the people gathered around him, and he sat down to teach them. The teachers of the law and the Pharisees brought in a woman caught in adultery. They made her stand before the group and said to Jesus, "Teacher, this woman was caught in the act of adultery. In the law Moses commanded us to stone such women. Now what do you say?" They were using this question as a trap, in order to have a basis for accusing him. But Jesus bent down and started to write on the ground with his finger. When they kept on questioning him, he straightened up and said to them, "Let any one of you who is without sin be the first to throw a stone at her." Again he stooped down and wrote on the ground. At this, those who heard began to go away one at a time, the older ones first, until only Jesus was left, with the woman still standing there. Jesus straightened up and asked her, "Woman,

where are they? Has no one condemned you?" "No one, sir," she said. "Then neither do I condemn you," Jesus declared. "Go now and leave your life of sin." (vv. 2-11)

Obviously, we don't know the back story to this encounter. We don't know how this woman has been caught in the act of adultery. Maybe she was set up. But the scribes and the Pharisees—the religious leaders of the day—bring this woman to Jesus, and they say to him, "In the law Moses commanded us to stone such women. Now what do you say?" Interestingly enough, these guys are half-right. Leviticus 20:10 and Deuteronomy 22:22 both indicate that adulterers must be put to death as part of the commands designed to keep God's people holy and set apart for God. Now, this law is troubling in its own right, but we do well to note that each passage requires that *both* the man *and* the woman caught in adultery be put to death. So, in bringing only the woman to be stoned, we already see the Pharisees perpetrating a serious injustice. Sadly, this was typical of the disempowered state of women in that culture—and typical in *any* culture in which sin is operative. As Genesis 3:16 predicts, where sin is at work, men dominate women. So it is unjust and yet predictable that this woman has been dragged out to be executed while, as far as we know, the man involved has already been let off the hook.

The gendered dynamic is not just incidental to this passage. At its ugliest, condemnation is a tool that the powerful use to marginalize the weak. Condemnation becomes a tool to *justify* marginalization, to explain why the social disadvantage of the weak makes sense—or is even "natural." Even so, the Pharisees know what the law demands. We can be troubled by the law itself and point out that the law says both partners in adultery should be stoned, but the text still says that *she* should be stoned. This woman is in a seriously tight spot. Not only is she condemned by these religious leaders, but also, as far as the text indicates, she is guilty of adultery. For all the mitigating social circumstances we might imagine, all the injustice present in the woman being condemned apart from the man, we have no indication that the situation is just one big misunderstanding.

Haven't we all been in this position? We do something we know isn't right, something that wrecks our relationships with the people we care about, with God, and with ourselves. Using the Bible's language, we would say that we have *sinned*. Maybe we've given in to an addiction we struggle with. Maybe a desire—for money, for power, for sex—has gotten the best of us. Maybe our basic self-orientation has blinded us to the needs of others. Whatever it is, we all have experienced the realization that something is wrong and that the problem, at least in part, is *us*. Often, on the heels of this realization—or sometimes even before it's dawned on us—comes the wagging finger of another to *condemn*, to say not just that we have sinned but that we *are* sinners. This voice insists that a *sinner* is who we are who we'll always be.

Condemnation leaves no room for hope. That's how condemnation works. It alienates the condemned person and convinces the people doing the condemning that the evil they see in the world has nothing to do with them. This is why, as a society, we incarcerate criminals or, in the extreme, condemn them to death. We do so in order to convince ourselves that criminality is something wholly other and that of the two categories of people in the world—good and bad—"we" are the good people and "they" are the bad. That's what we, as a society, get from the harshness of our criminal justice system, what we get from a system that not only convicts people of crimes but also assigns them lifelong labels of *felon* or *ex-convict*. We condemn a few in order to separate ourselves from the sin we nevertheless know lives inside us. Condemnation serves to protect us from our sin that we can't admit to ourselves. It externalizes it and removes it from view. So, when we stand on the other side, when we stand condemned—especially if and when we know we're guilty—it cuts to the core of our self-understanding. If we've bought into this fundamentally misguided worldview—that someone is either good or bad—then the only way to preserve goodness in the world is to eradicate bad people by condemning them. But once we find ourselves condemned, we may join those condemning us in order to satisfy our corrupted sense of justice. That's the woman's predicament—and, so often, ours as well.

Jesus has his own dilemma: If he lets the woman off the hook, he looks like he's "soft on crime," as it were, and he's a "lawbreaker"—which the Pharisees already suspect. (And, if we're honest, according to the letter of the law, that's probably a fair critique of Jesus. Jesus is quite willing to break a law for the sake of a higher purpose.) Letting her off would only further confirm the growing suspicion that Jesus is, in fact, a loosey-goosey libertine without regard for religious law. But if he lets these men go through with the stoning, he allows the poor woman to die. As we see later in the story, Jesus' primary interest is in the woman, so he certainly doesn't want to see her executed. And, for what it's worth, if he condones the stoning, he's breaking *Roman* law, which reserves capital punishment for the Romans themselves.

Ultimately, Jesus is in quite the bind, and that's exactly what the religious leaders want. These guys have gotten a sense of Jesus' MO, and they're suspicious about this religious teacher who hangs out with sinners way more than he should. They're suspicious of his morals, his character, and what would happen to society if his expansive embrace became the normal way of the world. Are we sometimes suspicious of Jesus in this way? Do we worry he's too lenient? That he's "Buddy Jesus," down with whatever, undoing everything we've learned about what's right and wrong? Perhaps. Though my hunch is that in our culture, we're much more likely to have the opposite concern because religious leaders have gotten their hands on Jesus and molded him in their own image. Perhaps we worry that Jesus is all too ready to condemn sinners.

I think we get this impression of Jesus as a harsh and condemning judge largely because of how many vocal Christians portray him: Jesus is invoked in our culture as the enemy of any number of "immoral" things. And though what counts as "immoral" changes from person to person, sometimes it seems like those lists are basically just a description of the cultural or political enemies of whoever's taken it upon themselves to define Jesus' likes and dislikes. At any rate, we have a sense that Jesus is a pretty stern fellow with some pretty strict rules, all too ready to condemn anyone who colors outside the lines. Of course, this is not the Jesus we find in this story—but neither do we get "Buddy Jesus." Instead, Jesus pursues a *third* way.

The scribes and the Pharisees present this dilemma to Jesus to set a trap for him. And what does Jesus do? The Bible says, "Jesus bent down and wrote with his finger on the ground." Jesus does this twice in the passage, perhaps to diffuse the tension of the situation. Imagine the scene: Jesus is teaching in the temple. People are everywhere. All of a sudden, the scribes and the Pharisees come to Jesus, accompanied by a crowd. They demand that Jesus preside over an impromptu stoning right then and there. There's this sense of urgency, of crisis. But all Jesus does is bend down and write or draw on the ground. He is unmoved by their sense of crisis. In this moment, Jesus offers them time to consider what's *really* going on here and whether they're *really* doing what God would have them do. And perhaps Jesus is taking a moment for himself in the middle of the madness—to pray, to listen for God.

When we compare Jesus' actions with that of the scribes and Pharisees, the differences are striking: The scribes and Pharisees are hurried—in fact, they're trying to create a crisis and use it to their advantage. In the face of that crisis, Jesus is nonetheless deliberate, unwilling to fall into their manufactured sense of urgency. The scribes and Pharisees merely use the woman for the sake of their test, whereas Jesus is actually interested in the woman herself, in her plight, and in her well-being. The scribes and Pharisees present themselves as concerned with the law of Moses, but this is giving them too much credit. By and large, they're concerned with identifying the woman as a rule-breaker and seeing her punished. Jesus, on the other hand, is concerned with rule-breakers in general: how they're treated, what happens to them, and what their futures look like. Instead of being hurried, Jesus takes the time to slow down and get God's perspective.

Jesus takes his time, giving the opportunity for those around him to pause, but they keep insisting on receiving an answer. So Jesus, centered in who he is and what God would have him do, stands up and says a few words: "Let any one of you who is without sin be the first to throw a stone at her." What a radical statement! In one sentence, Jesus both upholds Moses' law of execution and assures that no one will be executed. After all, Jesus phrases this sentence as a command to stone the woman, to follow through on Moses' law. But Jesus gives a *procedure* for how this stoning should happen: The first stone should be thrown by someone without sin. With these words, Jesus bends down again and writes on the ground, to give the scribes and Pharisees time to consider what it is that God is doing in that moment, to consider whether they can be the first to throw a stone, to consider whether *anyone* could be so qualified. And the text tells us that one by one—beginning with the oldest (and, presumably, the wisest)—each man recognizes that he is not qualified to condemn.

Eventually, Jesus is left alone with the woman—because Jesus *is* without sin. This woman, in her sin, is fundamentally other than Jesus. It *is* within Jesus' rights to condemn her. It is within Jesus' rights to condemn—period. But Jesus never sides with condemnation and exclusion. Standing up, Jesus asks her, "Woman, where are they? Has no one condemned you?" In this moment, we suddenly realize that if Jesus forbids all earthly condemnation—if we, who are sinners, can no longer condemn other sinners—then it must follow that we can no longer *be* condemned by others. Imagine all those voices from social media, from our families, from our workplaces, from our schools, from our churches and faith communities, and from inside our own heads that condemn, and then imagine them *silenced* by Jesus' rule. Legitimate condemnation can come only from those without sin. In other words, when we need to see past our actions and understand our fundamental identity, when we need to hear who we are rather than just what we've done, the only voice that should count is the voice of Jesus.

Then, Jesus, the one with every right to condemn her, the one without sin, says, "Then neither do I condemn you." In relinquishing his right to condemn, Jesus, having excluded all earthly condemnation, forgoes heavenly condemnation as well. Rather than pronounce her a "sinner" for all time, Jesus instead calls her forward with words that explain why he does not condemn: "Go now and leave your life of sin."

Jesus' words offer hope—and they offer the opportunity for transformation. The religious leaders' method of expunging sin involves getting rid of sinners because as far as the religious leaders are concerned, once a sinner always a sinner—it's an identity issue for them. Not so with Jesus. Jesus has hope for transformation. And that hope for transformation articulates the core of what Jesus offers us instead of condemnation.

· · · · · ·

In our culture, we don't distinguish between conviction and condemnation. We don't distinguish between conviction that tells the truth about what we've done and condemnation that extends the truth about what we've done into an ultimate definition of who we are. Condemnation takes conviction to its illogical extreme. Condemnation draws conclusions about *identity* from conviction's data of *conduct*. And that's just not how identity and conduct relate. But our culture can't tell these two fundamentally different activities apart. We're caught between two opposed but balanced social dysfunctions when it comes to dealing with the sin in our lives. On the one hand, we have the unforgiving self-righteousness of our culture that turns every conviction into condemnation. On the other, in a desire to defend ourselves from this unrelenting attack on our very identities, we try to rid ourselves from condemnation by sloughing off any sense of conviction as well. But the truth gets lost in the shuffle. In contrast, Jesus distinguishes between conviction and condemnation, saying both, "Neither do I condemn you" and "Go now and leave your life of sin." Jesus can convict without condemning, and he invites us to live in the health and freedom that comes from a life marked both by freedom from condemnation *and* by the regular presence of conviction of sin in our lives.

Jesus does not condemn us, though it would be entirely within his rights to do so. Jesus sees us as we actually are and has the moral high ground from which to pronounce judgment on us but chooses not to. However, neither does Jesus say that our flaws and our sin are no big deal. Jesus not only loves us *as* we are and *where* we are but also loves us *forward*. From the lives we're leading at the moment to the lives we're called to lead, Jesus loves us too much to leave us where we are. In Jesus' eyes, we are not, at our core, sinners—though we do sin. For this reason, Jesus often spends time with people who others call "sinners." Whereas others only see people through the lens of what they've done and where they've been, Jesus sees who they are, where they've been, *and* who they were created to be. Jesus sees us as we were created to be, and his call to follow him is nothing less than a call to become our truest selves—who we were made to be.

What Jesus offers us in seeing us as we are but also as God made us to be is something we can offer one another. This way of seeing is crucially important to the way we live together in community. We can love one another as Jesus loves us, and we also can love one another *forward*. It's not easy. It's not always comfortable. But it's part of helping one another grow.

· · · · · ·

Maureen and her husband, Tom, have been friends of mine for almost twenty years. They have taught me so much about what it means to follow Jesus, particularly when the going gets tough. Maureen has the gift of speaking the truth even when it's uncomfortable. On more than one occasion, when I've needed to hear the truth, Maureen has spoken it to me.

On one such occasion a few years ago, I needed to hear the difficult truth about my relationship with Tom. Over the years, our friendship has involved a bit of good-natured ribbing. I often tell people that sarcasm is my love language, and I love Tom, so we would tease each other in the way that friends sometimes do. But over time, the teasing became more and more one-sided, and, eventually, Maureen came to me with a concern. She told me that the jokes had stopped being funny for Tom; they were actually hurtful. "Matt," she told me, "it's *unbecoming* of you to behave this way." I'll never forget that word, *unbecoming*. That's what drove her to come to me—not a sense that my sin revealed who I really was but a deep conviction that my actions were preventing me from being who I really am, a beloved child of God. Her words didn't "cure" me. I still hurt people I care about through what strikes me as a good-natured joke. But I have learned from Maureen to take those moments seriously, to seek forgiveness and reconciliation.

When I think of what genuine friendship looks like, Maureen's frank honesty, calling me to be better, comes to mind. We participate in God's work of naming sin in others' lives not because we think sin defines who they are but because, like Jesus, we are committed to others' true identities as beautiful pieces of God's handiwork. This is the difference between condemnation, which seeks to define and exclude us, and conviction, which reaches us where we are and loves us forward—and it's important to keep this difference in mind as we confront our sin and the sin of others.

· · · · · ·

As we engage with Jesus' question—"Has no one condemned you?"—let's consider those people by whom we feel condemned, perhaps our coworkers, our family, church members, or ourselves. Imagine Jesus inviting them to cast the first stone—but only if they are without sin. Watch as, one by one, they drop their stones and walk away. This is how Jesus sees us and those who would condemn us. Jesus disarms them. Only then can we hear anew Jesus' question to us: "Where did they go? Has no one condemned you?" Jesus invites us to live free from the condemnation of others and even of ourselves.

But how about those whom we condemn? We also must imagine those people we all too easily condemn—people unlike us, people who condemn us, people whose sin looks so much like our own that they upset our self-righteousness. Imagine Jesus inviting us to cast the first stone—but only if we are without sin. Watch as, one by one, we drop the stones intended for someone else. Consider the release of condemnation that comes with each dropped stone. Look at Jesus' face as we walk away. Hear again Jesus' question, addressed this time to each person we've been tempted to condemn: "Has no one condemned you?" Let's accept Jesus' invitation to live as people who no longer condemn. Only then can we begin to hear and act on Jesus' words spoken to us: "Go now and leave your life of sin"—beginning with the sin of condemnation.

Monday, Week 2

. . . .

Read John 8:2-11.

At dawn [Jesus] appeared again in the temple courts, where all the people gathered around him, and he sat down to teach them. The teachers of the law and the Pharisees brought in a woman caught in adultery. They made her stand before the group and said to Jesus, "Teacher, this woman was caught in the act of adultery. In the Law Moses commanded us to stone such women. Now what do you say?" They were using this question as a trap, in order to have a basis for accusing him. But Jesus bent down and started to write on the ground with his finger. When they kept on questioning him, he straightened up and said to them, "Let any one of you who is without sin be the first to throw a stone at her." Again he stooped down and wrote on the ground. At this, those who heard began to go away one at a time, the older ones first, until only Jesus was left, with the woman still standing there. Jesus straightened up and asked her, "Woman, where are they? **Has no one condemned you?**" "No one, sir," she said. "Then neither do I condemn you," Jesus declared. "Go now and leave your life of sin."

Reflection

Dragged to Jesus in order to expose him as a flagrant who doesn't care about the law, the woman is a mere prop for the religious officials. But Jesus sees her differently. Jesus concedes that the religious law says she deserves to be stoned, but he suggests a particular method for the execution: Let the one without sin be the first to throw a stone. One after another, the men walk away, and the woman is left alone with Jesus. The only one who could condemn her by his own rule, Jesus nevertheless withholds condemnation. "Has no one condemned you?" he asks. Jesus' question captures the core of God's extravagant grace. With this question, we're invited to open our eyes, look around, and consider whether Jesus' forgiveness indeed has freed us from condemnation.

Continue the Conversation

Jesus: Has no one condemned you?

Me: ....

....

....

....

....

....

....

....

....

....

....

....

....

....

Tuesday, Week 2

· · · · · · · · · · · ·

Read Luke 7:36-47.

When one of the Pharisees invited Jesus to have dinner with him, he went to the Pharisee's house and reclined at the table. A woman in that town who lived a sinful life learned that Jesus was eating at the Pharisee's house, so she came there with an alabaster jar of perfume. As she stood behind him at his feet weeping, she began to wet his feet with her tears. Then she wiped them with her hair, kissed them and poured perfume on them. When the Pharisee who had invited him saw this, he said to himself, "If this man were a prophet, he would know who is touching him and what kind of woman she is—that she is a sinner." Jesus answered him, "Simon, I have something to tell you." "Tell me, teacher," he said. "Two people owed money to a certain moneylender. One owed him five hundred denarii, and the other fifty. Neither of them had the money to pay him back, so he forgave the debts of both. Now which of them will love him more?" Simon replied, "I suppose the one who had the bigger debt forgiven." "You have judged correctly," Jesus said. Then he turned toward the woman and said to Simon, **"Do you see this woman?** I came into your house. You did not give me any water for my feet, but she wet my feet with her tears and wiped them with her hair. You did not give me a kiss, but this woman, from the time I entered, has not stopped kissing my feet. You did not put oil on my head, but she has poured perfume on my feet. Therefore, I tell you, her many sins have been forgiven—as her great love has shown. But whoever has been forgiven little loves little."

Reflection

Jesus wants to know if Simon truly sees the woman before him. Our world is full of people like this woman—people who we don't really see or see merely as stereotypes of one kind or another. These people may be the homeless, the poor, addicts, convicts, or perhaps folks who identify with a particular race, ethnicity, religion, gender, sexual orientation, or political party. Jesus invites us to consider what it would be like to see these people as they are. Often, when we're willing to let God open our eyes to see others as they really are, we find that we have something important to learn from them about how to follow Jesus—just as Simon has something to learn from this nameless woman.

Continue the Conversation

Jesus: Do you see this woman?

Me: ....

....

....

....

....

....

....

....

....

....

....

....

....

....

Wednesday, Week 2

. . . .

Read Matthew 7:1-5.

"Do not judge, or you too will be judged. For in the same way you judge others, you will be judged, and with the measure you use, it will be measured to you. **Why do you look at the speck of sawdust in your brother's eye and pay no attention to the plank in your own eye?** How can you say to your brother, 'Let me take the speck out of your eye,' when all the time there is a plank in your own eye? You hypocrite, first take the plank out of your own eye, and then you will see clearly to remove the speck from your brother's eye."

Reflection

The grace we receive when Jesus withholds condemnation—even when we're caught red-handed in our sin—is something we're expected to share with others. Nevertheless, we're constantly caught up in others' shortcomings while we remain oblivious to our own. Jesus' questions don't merely point out our blatant hypocrisy; they also remind us that we cannot be useful to others without removing our own hindrances to wholeness first. Jesus' question provides a moment for self-diagnosis. If we take seriously our own brokenness, Jesus' grace and transforming presence can remove the issues that distort our vision and prevent us from helping others find their own healing. Let's invite Jesus to look at our sin—those barriers that interfere with our relationships with others, with God, and with ourselves—and trust that he can bring us healing and make us an agent of others' healing as well. For even when Jesus' questions challenge and convict us, they never condemn us.

Continue the Conversation

Jesus: Why do you look at the speck of sawdust in your brother's eye and pay no attention to the plank in your own eye?

Me: ....

....

....

....

....

....

....

....

....

....

....

....

....

Thursday, Week 2

. . . .

Read Luke 6:32-36.

"**If you love those who love you, what credit is that to you?** Even sinners love those who love them. And if you do good to those who are good to you, what credit is that to you? Even sinners do that. And if you lend to those from whom you expect repayment, what credit is that to you? Even sinners lend to sinners, expecting to be repaid in full. But love your enemies, do good to them, and lend to them without expecting to get anything back. Then your reward will be great, and you will be children of the Most High, because he is kind to the ungrateful and wicked. Be merciful, just as your Father is merciful."

Reflection

Jesus' love for us is reckless, and he withholds condemnation even when we deserve it. This reckless love ought to be our own paradigm of love. In this passage, Jesus exposes the feeble brand of love for which we so often want a pat on the back. In Jesus' day, perhaps even more blatantly than in our own, the social hierarchy was built upon exchanges of favors between social equals—that is, the rich exchanging gifts with other rich people. Jesus says this doesn't pass for love. If we want to be people marked by love, we need to love our enemies and those who can't repay us. These, of course, are precisely the people we don't want to love, but, then again, our relationship with Jesus is hardly an exchange of honors between equals. As the Bible tells us, Jesus extends us grace when we stand amid our sin. Let's consider what it would look like—and cost—to love like Jesus.

Continue the Conversation

Jesus: If you love those who love you, what credit is that to you?

Me: ....

....

....

....

....

....

....

....

....

....

....

....

....

Friday, Week 2

· · · · · · · · · · · ·

Read Matthew 18:21-35.

Peter came to Jesus and asked, "Lord, how many times shall I forgive my brother or sister who sins against me? Up to seven times?" Jesus answered, "I tell you, not seven times, but seventy-seven times. Therefore, the kingdom of heaven is like a king who wanted to settle accounts with his servants. As he began the settlement, a man who owed him ten thousand bags of gold was brought to him. Since he was not able to pay, the master ordered that he and his wife and his children and all that he had be sold to repay the debt. At this the servant fell on his knees before him. 'Be patient with me,' he begged, 'and I will pay back everything.' The servant's master took pity on him, canceled the debt and let him go. But when that servant went out, he found one of his fellow servants who owed him a hundred silver coins. He grabbed him and began to choke him. 'Pay back what you owe me!' he demanded. His fellow servant fell to his knees and begged him, 'Be patient with me, and I will pay it back.' But he refused. Instead, he went off and had the man thrown into prison until he could pay the debt. When the other servants saw what had happened, they were outraged and went and told their master everything that had happened. Then the master called the servant in. 'You wicked servant,' he said, 'I canceled all that debt of yours because you begged me to. **Shouldn't you have had mercy on your fellow servant just as I had on you?'** In anger his master handed him over to the jailers to be tortured, until he should pay back all he owed. This is how my heavenly Father will treat each of you unless you forgive your brother or sister from your heart."

Reflection

The king's question in the story becomes Jesus' question to us. Jesus reminds us that we only receive forgiveness when we also extend it to others—not because God is vindictive (despite the admittedly harsh language used to describe the master in this parable) but because of natural consequence. Jesus' question invites us to consider the ways that not offering forgiveness can damage our own lives. Who should we forgive today?

Continue the Conversation

Jesus: Shouldn't you have had mercy on your fellow servant just as I had on you?

Me: ....

....

....

....

....

....

....

....

....

....

....

....

....

....

Why Do You Worry?

A few years ago, I found myself in the middle of perhaps the most stressful season of my life. Most of the stress came from work. My colleagues and I were writing a grant, and I was doing most of the drafting. It was a brutal process, trying to juggle at once the overlap of budget spreadsheets and descriptions of project activities, thinking about the intellectual content, then the budgetary impact, then the staffing questions, then each funding source's particular interests. During the worst of it, my colleagues and I would work until 3 a.m. one night and be back at it the next morning at 8:30 a.m. Ultimately, my future employment depended on the success of the grant. No grant, no job. No job, no money. No money—well, that would be a problem. But more than that, this grant-writing job was the first one I had secured out of graduate school. What would it mean if I were to *fail*?

My colleagues and I had reason to believe we would succeed, but even that knowledge offered me no solace. I wondered, even if we succeeded, would any of the jobs we were proposing in the grant really be *me*? I had given up teaching for the semester in order to write the grant—in some ways that was the hardest part of the experience. I had given up teaching at the university, and I was on sabbatical from the church. So, amid having taken a break from teaching, the one thing

I know most gives me life, I was also asking myself urgently, *Who am I?* I was pretty sure I wasn't a grant writer, but was there some version of me—some more fully actualized "Matt"—at the end of this long, dark tunnel? I couldn't sleep. I found myself lost in cycles of despair, anxiety, and panic.

· · · · · ·

Worry can hijack our lives, and we've all experienced it. Jesus' question to us in this chapter is simply this: "Why do you worry?"

> "Do not worry about your life, what you will eat or drink; or about your body, what you will wear. Is not life more than food, and the body more than clothing? Look at the birds of the air; they do not sow or reap or store away in barns, and yet your heavenly Father feeds them. Are you not much more valuable than they? Can any one of you by worrying add a single hour to your life? And why do you worry about clothes? See how the flowers of the field grow. They do not labor or spin. Yet I tell you that not even Solomon in all his splendor was dressed like one of these. If that is how God clothes the grass of the field, which is here today and tomorrow is thrown into the fire, will he not much more clothe you—you of little faith? So do not worry, saying, 'What shall we eat?' or 'What shall we drink?' or 'What shall we wear?' For the pagans run after all these things, and your heavenly Father knows that you need them. But seek first his kingdom and his righteousness, and all these things will be given to you as well. Therefore do not worry about tomorrow, for tomorrow will worry about itself. Each day has enough trouble of its own." (Matt. 6:25-34)

Jesus has a lot to say about why we *needn't* worry, but I don't think that his question mocks our worry. Jesus doesn't think we *need* to worry and would like to relieve us of the overwhelming sense of worry that often chokes the joy out of our lives. But, as a first step, Jesus genuinely wants to know *why* we worry.

As a way of leading us into the conversation that Jesus wants to have with us, let's consider three answers we have for Jesus' question and further discern how Jesus might respond to us, given what Jesus has to say in the rest of the passage. There are certainly more than three worries that afflict our lives, but these three categories capture a lot of what keeps us up at night and add anxiety to our lives. We worry about (1) material goods, (2) success in our various vocations and projects, and (3) success in our most important project—"achieving ourselves." Each of these worries invites Jesus to ask *another* question, and we'll collect these additional questions as we discuss this passage of scripture. Depending on how we answer Jesus' first question—"Why do you worry?"—we may find ourselves answering one of Jesus' later questions as well.

· · · · · ·

Let's start with the answer that's front and center in the passage. Sometimes we worry about the basic things of life: food, drink, clothes, and shelter. That is, we worry about material provision: Will we have enough? Where will our basic necessities come from? Are our sources reliable? For the original audience of this passage, these are legitimate worries. Jesus' audience is, by and large, composed of rural peasants and a few tradespeople. They don't always know where their next meal is coming from. Basic needs aren't something Jesus' earliest followers can count on. For far too many people in the world today, this continues to be the case.

To be clear, when Jesus tells these folks not to worry, he's not doing so because he doesn't care about their poverty or because he doesn't think material deprivation is a big deal. Material insecurity is an evil, something to be eradicated whenever and wherever it shows itself. "Don't worry" is never a sufficient response to the poverty of others. Jesus spends a lot of time in his ministry teaching about the responsibility that the rich have toward the poor, to say nothing of the times he miraculously meets people's material needs. (The last of this week's exercises will focus on one of these stories and the responsibility Jesus says we have in participating in providing for the poor.) Material insecurity—whether others' or our own—ought to elicit legitimate concern for ourselves and for others. Nevertheless, even to those in dire straits, Jesus warns against all-consuming worry and offers an invitation: "Don't worry; your heavenly Father cares for you. See yourself beyond that which you lack. Seek first the kingdom of God, and God will provide for your needs." This invitation offers dignity to those who are impoverished. Jesus refuses to reduce the poor to their poverty; he recognizes that the universal human striving for transcendence, for meaning, and for purpose do not vanish when hunger sets in. After all, many of the world's great spiritual insights have come from people who were desperately poor by modern standards. The sturdiness of human dignity in the face of material insecurity demands that we act to relieve poverty whenever and wherever we can.

I have had the privilege of not experiencing this sort of insecurity. Not knowing where my next paycheck would come from? Sure, I've been there. Not sure where my next meal would come from? That hasn't been my experience, thanks be to God. However, I can't say that I haven't worried about material things. Really, in modern life, we've boiled down all these concerns to just one: concern about *money*. Our economy's number one product—more than cars or computers or cell phones—is precisely that: worry about money. We're told we don't have enough, that we will never have enough. In part, this is because of the slipperiness of the idea of "enough." For many of us, we're not worried about having something to eat, something to wear, or a roof over our heads. Our concern is about having enough in order to eat the sort of food we want to eat, enough to wear the "right" sort of clothes, and to live in the sort of house that will facilitate the sort of life that we want for ourselves and our children. We worry that we haven't saved what we'll need to have "enough" long after we're no longer able to draw a paycheck. And we learn, bit by bit, to inflate our sense of what counts as "enough" such that we have a very real sense that, regardless of how much we have, we may be living right on the edge of what is "enough."

An acquaintance of mine, a CEO of a medium-sized corporation, attends an annual retreat with other executives of similarly sized companies for networking. The retreat is held out in the middle of nowhere, so on the first day, everyone arrives at a small airfield near the conference site. Most people fly in on charter jets since no commercial flights fly to this tiny airport. These are the first folks to arrive. Then come the people who fly in on their own planes—planes they actually own. One by one, these planes land—small turboprops and eventually a couple small jets. A chorus of oohs and ahhs erupt when the private jets start landing. While my acquaintance is chatting up one of guys who flew in on his own jet—hearing his rags-to-riches story of how he had built his business from nothing—an enormous plane the size of a commercial airliner arrives, carrying one of the wealthiest retreat attendees. The rags-to-riches CEO—the owner of one of the small private jets—with mouth agape, leans over to my acquaintance and says, "I have never felt so poor in my life." If even a private jet can feel like poverty, we ought to stop hoping that we'll ever be free of worry by getting more stuff.

Amid a runaway sense of what ought to be "enough," we have an opportunity to stop and think about God's promise to provide for our necessities. We can consider the birds of the air and the flowers of the field, how God always supplies them with what they need. We can assure ourselves that God has similarly promised to supply us with what we need—and we would be right to do so. God is generous, and we can depend on God for what we need. When we live in dependence on God's provision, we will find God extravagantly generous.

At the same time, we have to be 100 percent clear that this has *nothing* to do with God promising to provide us with what would count for us as "enough." This has serious consequences for the efficacy of God's promises in alleviating our worry. Because if God promises us what we need and we're worried instead about having "enough," then God's promise of sufficiency can't relieve our anxiety about the excess we so eagerly desire. Instead, we have to let Jesus ask us another question, and we ought to consider it at least as carefully as we consider the first: "Is not life more than food, and the body more than clothing?"

Right from the start, Jesus cuts to the heart of the matter. Our worries depend upon and project a vision of life that is fundamentally false—namely, a vision that portrays that life is simply about food and the body simply about clothing. Modulating our desires—not expecting too much or too little—is not the point. If we've misconstrued our lives as being fundamentally about material things, our worrying about what we need, what we want, what we consider "enough"— obsession with any of it—simply misses the point. Instead, Jesus suggests we view life this way: "Seek first [God's] kingdom." The kingdom of God, Jesus teaches, is what life is really about. Now, there's a lot that could be said here— the concept of the kingdom of God is deep and wide. But, briefly, the ancient church planter, Paul, defines the kingdom in Romans 14:17 (a passage that is reminiscent of Jesus' own teachings): "The kingdom of God is not a matter of eating and drinking, but of righteousness, peace and joy in the Holy Spirit." The kingdom of God is a vision of life that moves far beyond material things like food and drink. The kingdom is justice (another translation for the Greek word often rendered "righteousness"), peace, and joy in and through God's presence, the flourishing of individuals, communities, nations, and the whole world. It is a matter of true justice, peace, and joy. This is the kingdom: human life in its fullness because it is richly caught up in the life of God. *That's* what life is really for.

If we seek first the true life, then all these things—our material *needs*—will be given to us as well. When the kingdom has the place of priority, even those material things become more than they are in themselves. Suddenly, they are *gifts* of a God who draws near to us. Once we get our perspective right, once we seek first the kingdom, rather than worrying about material things, the material things of life become a venue for encountering the living God. Not only is life more than food and the body more than clothes, but also food is more than simply food—it is bread from heaven. Drink is more than drink; it is a sacrament of the Living Water Jesus provides. Clothes are more than clothes; they are physical reminders of the way in which we are wrapped in the arms of God. As my friend and colleague Miroslav Volf writes in his book *Flourishing: Why We Need Religion in a Globalized World*, once we see the material world for what it is—a gift from the God who is love—"literally every good and beautiful thing shimmers with an aura both vibrantly real and undetectable to our five senses. Each thing in the world is more than itself and just so a source of deep and many-layered pleasure."

So why do we worry?

· · · · · ·

The second cause of worry in our life is the "success" that we seek in the various projects in our lives. This source of worry has had a particularly strong hold on my life. I already mentioned that fall when I was drafting a grant, but there have been others as well: when I applied to graduate school, when I taught my first lecture course in graduate school, when I first planted a church, and so on.

What ties all these seasons of my life together is this: For better and for worse, I was invested heavily in the outcomes of my projects. I say for better and for worse because it really was a mixed bag. I want to be invested in the world, invested in people, and invested in projects that *matter*. I care enough about these things to pour my time, my energy, and my heart into them. I care about what happens at the end. But it's terrifying as well because, unless we're under some sort of self-aggrandizing delusion, once we get ourselves invested in a project, a goal, and an outcome, we realize that our hoped-for outcome isn't under our control. Maybe it is in part but never completely. Success depends on so many factors outside our control—the cooperation of others, the luck of the draw, the fickle opinions of those who are in positions to judge our success. This means that if we're aiming for success, worry becomes an inescapable reality of life. And it's not just that our worry is *inevitable*, it's that our worry is *justified*. If our goal is success, we're right to worry because success is not in our hands.

Jesus again anticipates this problem and has a secondary question ready to address it: "Can any one of you by worrying add a single hour to your life?" From the start, Jesus recognizes what we so often fail to see: Our experience of worry ironically exposes the cause of our worry and, at the same time, its uselessness. We worry because we recognize that things we care about are fundamentally out of our control. Even the most fundamental goal of our biological existence—the extension of our life itself—is beyond our control. But the fact that the outcomes that we so desire are beyond our control demonstrates just how useless our worry is, which means that, as with material goods, *getting what we want is hardly the solution to our worry*. We got that grant I was so worried about, but it wasn't the solution to my worry. Counting on universal "success" in all our projects is hardly a recipe to do away with worry.

What will work, however, is this: Seek first the kingdom of God and his righteousness. Seek first the *kingdom*. And, in particular, the righteousness—the *justice*—of God. We can't focus on life going well; that was the first trap, and it's out of our control. We must focus first on *leading* our life well, giving God authority to shape how we exercise our agency. We must focus on righteousness and on justice, which means seeking not *success* but *obedience*. And that will change our lives. God has turned my life upside-down through this one simple swap: Instead of aiming for success, I aim for obedience. While success is never entirely in my hands, obedience always is. Obedience is strictly about my response to Jesus' call to follow him. And, when I can train my focus this way, the result, as Jesus says, is freedom from worry.

With this approach to life, I've found that I have to repent a lot more because I'm no better at obeying Jesus than I am at "succeeding" in my various projects. In fact, I may be worse at it. But the obedience paradigm transforms how I deal with coming up short. When we aim for success and come up short, the world calls it *failure*, and our only possible response is regret and trying harder next time. Neither of those is much fun. But when we fall short of obedience, Jesus calls it *sin*, and our response can be repentance, receiving forgiveness, and being transformed. Suffice to say that obedience is the way to live. Aiming for obedience in my life has meant judging days not by what got accomplished but by an hour-by-hour or even moment-by-moment sense of whether I'm being obedient to what Jesus has asked of me. When I'm able to maintain that posture, it changes everything. I'm able to see my days not as sets of tasks that must be accomplished but as time that ought to be stewarded well for God's purpose. When I get to the end of a day hopelessly overloaded with tasks, I take solace in having stewarded my hours well and obeyed Jesus' prompting—and receiving God's forgiveness and experiencing true release and freedom when that *wasn't* the case. Repentance and forgiveness beat regret and worry every time. Let's give up on success and aim for obedience instead.

• • • • • •

One final cause of worry is particular to this day and age and may be fundamental to everything else that makes us worry. It has to do with a peculiar task that we think we have responsibility for, a task that no previous generation of people understood to be theirs: the task of "achieving ourselves." I get this language from French sociologist Alain Ehrenberg in his book *The Weariness of the Self: Diagnosing the History of Depression in the Contemporary Age*. When the book came across my desk, what Ehrenberg described was immediately familiar to me—from my own life and from the lives of the students I teach. The situation is this: As modern people, we are told again and again that our destiny lies in our own hands. We get to decide who we want to be and where we want to go. Our possibilities are limitless; we can *be* anyone and *do* anything. We believe this about ourselves, and we teach these lessons to our children. This is the task that no previous generation considered their own—at least not to the same degree. In previous generations, who we *were* was determined by our family, community, or place in society. In some sense, the trajectory of the lives of previous generations was decided before they were born. Not so for us—at least, this is what we believe.

This mindset holds good news and bad news. On the one hand, the belief that we can be anything and do anything is one of the chief goods that modernity has delivered to us: freedom to be and to do as we like. Everything is possible; nothing is forbidden. On the other hand, we receive a potentially crushing responsibility with this freedom: Our very selves—once given to us as a gift by our family, our communities, and our ancestors—go from being gifts to becoming tasks. This is our ironic modern "birthright": the right to receive nothing from birth. We no longer start our lives as selves. Rather, we are responsible to *achieve ourselves*. And we don't do this work in isolation; we are forced to achieve ourselves in competition with one another. I'm free to become whomever I want to be, but the results of my self-achievement always will be compared to the results of others. Worse yet, often this comparison happens on social media where my comprehensive view of my own success and failure will never measure up to the most impressive fraction of others' lives that they choose to share.

Recently, my daughter has been obsessed with the movie *Moana*. It's a classic postmodern movie: Moana's main task is to discover who she is beyond who her family says she is and beyond who her community wants her to be—though not apart from these (that's the *post*modern part). It's a wearying task, even for a fictional Disney hero, a complex negotiation among tradition, vocation, and personal impulse. The climax of the movie—which my daughter knows to belt out at the top of her lungs—is the title character's declaration: "I am Moana." By that point in the movie, this declaration has genuine context: She knows who she is—not merely through *discovery* but through the hard work of *crafting* herself. She has *achieved* herself. It's exhilarating to watch, as the children and adults who love the film can attest.

The sort of worry that can result from this crushing responsibility to achieve ourselves is perhaps the deepest worry of all. We worry that we're somehow missing *ourselves,* that we'll never find who we are and who we're meant to be. Phrased that way, this can sound like an affliction of the young—and, no doubt, this worry plagues those in adolescence and young adulthood. But it is no less potent later in life, when the concern becomes that we have *missed* ourselves. This worry looks less like an overwhelmed shopper in a store with too many choices and more like buyer's remorse. If the achievement of the self is our most significant consumer choice, it is subject to the highest degree of what philosopher Barry Schwartz calls "the paradox of choice": the disappointment that comes from the sense that, with so many choices, we should be able to find something *perfect*. When it comes to our identity, we are told that we have an infinite array of possibilities to choose from. So if anything in our lives is less than perfect, we worry that we chose wrong or that we've failed at life's most central task.

In response, Jesus asks us, "Look at the birds of the air; they do not sow or reap or store away in barns, and yet your heavenly Father feeds them. Are you not much more valuable than they?" Jesus wants to know if we understand how valuable we are and if we know the *source* of our value. Our value comes from God—not from any sense of achievement, not from what we do or don't do, not from a sense of self we craft out of infinite possibilities. But how can we come to believe this fact and live with this knowledge as the very foundation of our lives?

· · · · · ·

Thinking back on my time writing that grant, I've realized that I not only worried about material needs and professional success but also, more than anything, I worried about what I was or was not learning about my identity. My greatest concern was that, amid everything else, I was losing myself and that, somehow, I would fail to become the person I was called to be. Each semester I watch my students wrestle with similar issues. Many worry that the burden of achieving themselves is somehow beyond what they can accomplish. I sit with them as they worry that the central task of their lives is both inalienably their responsibility and above their pay grade. Even so, I've had a number of students who have taught me about finding rescue from this overwhelming anxiety.

One student, after thoughtfully wrestling with this existential worry, concluded that the only way she could be free of anxiety was to believe that God was real and had promised to provide everything she needed—including her sense of identity, meaning, and purpose. This realization didn't come suddenly, but after years of heartache and genuine struggle and a semester of discerning the source of true life, she felt genuinely convicted of God's reality and goodness. It was startling for me, as someone who often struggles to trust in God's goodness, to hear the genuine, earnest certainty that she had suddenly found. God was present and had promised all she needed; she had no doubt about it. She was also quite candid about not having everything figured out, and she wasn't sure of a religious tradition that would help her continue her journey with the God she discovered. Other than as a cosmic provider, she wasn't sure of what else she could say about who God was. But her face shone with the confidence founded in assurance from a God who had promised to take care of her no matter what. That faith lifted years of anxiety from her shoulders. It was beautiful—and humbling—to witness.

Another student—one from a Christian background—came to a similar conclusion after his own wrestling: The only way to have the life he wanted was to believe that God loved him unconditionally. The only problem? He wasn't sure he could believe it. Though he was utterly convinced that only the unconditional love of God could serve as an adequate foundation for the sort of life he wanted, he was equally certain that belief in that sort of love was beyond what he could muster. He knew he needed this love—wanted to believe it was true—but he couldn't make himself believe it. In the midst of trying to write his final paper for the course—his vision of a life truly worth living—he reached out in something of a panic. Which was "his" vision: the life founded on divine love he hoped was possible or the life of existential doubt he feared was inevitably his? On the night before the paper was due, deep in the basement of the library, he and I wrestled with that question together. As we went back and forth, it became clear that neither side of his dilemma could portray his vision adequately without losing something of the truth of where he was at in that moment. His final paper for the course was a tragic ode to a divine love that he had never experienced but knew would make all the difference in his life—if he could come to believe it were real. His journey was no less beautiful or humbling to witness.

Jesus isn't asking us questions in order to find out if we know the right answers. Jesus isn't quizzing us; he's trying to start a conversation. He's trying to forge and deepen a relationship. And, like any relationship, we take steps forward in intimacy only through honesty and dialogue. Jesus wants us to be honest with him about where we're at. If we're pretty sure that God is real and good but have little idea what Jesus has to do with all of that, we should be honest about that. If we *wish* we could believe that God loves us unconditionally but can't, we should say so. Perhaps the most honest answer to Jesus' question about worry is this: "I'm not sure if you are who you say you are." If that's where we are, that's what we need to be willing to tell him.

I remember the last thing I said late in the library that night with the student struggling with his final paper. I said, "I know it feels like you're in the horns of a dilemma. I know it feels impossible. But I have so much hope for you. Because you're being honest with God." The God I have come to know in Jesus honors that sort of honesty, that sort of candor. Not that it's easy, but Jesus is persistent with us when we're real with him.

Monday, Week 3

· · · · · · · · · · · ·

Read Matthew 6:25-34.

"Do not worry about your life, what you will eat or drink; or about your body, what you will wear. Is not life more than food, and the body more than clothes? Look at the birds of the air; they do not sow or reap or store away in barns, and yet your heavenly Father feeds them. Are you not much more valuable than they? Can any one of you by worrying add a single hour to your life? And **why do you worry** about clothes? See how the flowers of the field grow. They do not labor or spin. Yet I tell you that not even Solomon in all his splendor was dressed like one of these. If that is how God clothes the grass of the field, which is here today and tomorrow is thrown into the fire, will he not much more clothe you—you of little faith? So do not worry, saying, 'What shall we eat?' or 'What shall we drink?' or 'What shall we wear?' For the pagans run after all these things, and your heavenly Father knows that you need them. But seek first his kingdom and his righteousness, and all these things will be given to you as well. Therefore do not worry about tomorrow, for tomorrow will worry about itself. Each day has enough trouble of its own."

Reflection

This question reveals Jesus' basic orientation to time. Jesus lives in the moment for the sake of what lasts forever; he invites us to focus on the now for the sake of the eternal. Focusing on everything else—all the tomorrows to come—only serves to get us lost in worry. As a result, we may be ready to answer Jesus' question with a laundry list of reasons that we worry. For many of us, our worries are not nearly as fundamental as whether we will be able to eat or drink or have clothes to wear. Yet Jesus insists that God's provision means that even when our future is uncertain with regard to these basic necessities, we still need not worry. The world may tell us that we must chase after everything we need and desire in life, but Jesus says that God already knows what we need and is ready to provide for us.

Continue the Conversation

Jesus: Why do you worry?

Me: ....

....

....

....

....

....

....

....

....

....

....

....

....

....

Tuesday, Week 3

. . . .

Read Luke 10:1-9; 22:35.

The Lord appointed seventy-two others and sent them two by two ahead of him to every town and place where he was about to go. He told them, "The harvest is plentiful, but the workers are few. Ask the Lord of the harvest, therefore, to send out workers into his harvest field. Go! I am sending you out like lambs among wolves. Do not take a purse or bag or sandals; and do not greet anyone on the road. When you enter a house, first say, 'Peace to this house.' If someone who promotes peace is there, your peace will rest on them; if not, it will return to you. Stay there, eating and drinking whatever they give you, for the worker deserves his wages. Do not move around from house to house. When you enter a town and are welcomed, eat what is offered to you. Heal the sick who are there and tell them, 'The kingdom of God has come near to you.'" . . . Then Jesus asked them, **"When I sent you without purse, bag or sandals, did you lack anything?"** "Nothing," they answered.

Reflection

"I am sending you out like lambs among wolves"—a life following Jesus is apparently not supposed to be safe. There's risk inherent to this way of life, and Jesus sends out his followers in such a way that deliberately maximizes their exposure. They must depend on the people to whom they are sent: staying in others' homes, eating what others offer them. Jesus is teaching them that vulnerability is essential to their mission to proclaim and demonstrate that the kingdom of God—a kingdom built on justice, healing, forgiveness, and peace—is at hand. Yet, in the upside-down way in which God's kingdom works, even though they are exposed, even though they go without basic provisions, they nevertheless lack nothing. This risky adventure proves God's dedication to their well-being. Given that doing what God would have us do always entails risks, Jesus' question is worth considering. When we've taken risks to do what we thought was right, what happened? Did we ultimately lack what we needed? Did God provide?

Continue the Conversation

Jesus: When I sent you . . . did you lack anything?

Me: ....

....

....

....

....

....

....

....

....

....

....

....

....

Wednesday, Week 3

· · · · · · · · · · · ·

Read Mark 4:35-41.

That day when evening came, [Jesus] said to his disciples, "Let us go over to the other side." Leaving the crowd behind, they took him along, just as he was, in the boat. There were also other boats with him. A furious squall came up, and the waves broke over the boat, so that it was nearly swamped. Jesus was in the stern, sleeping on a cushion. The disciples woke him and said to him, "Teacher, don't you care if we drown?" He got up, rebuked the wind and said to the waves, "Quiet! Be still!" Then the wind died down and it was completely calm. He said to his disciples, **"Why are you so afraid?** Do you still have no faith?" They were terrified and asked each other, "Who is this? Even the wind and the waves obey him!"

Reflection

In this passage, Jesus' question comes in response to a pointed question posed by his disciples: "Don't you care?" Circumstances have so overwhelmed the disciples that they're starting to question their most basic belief about who Jesus is. They've seen him provide for them and for those around him. They've seen him heal people and give them freedom from spiritual forces that oppressed them. But the storm is enough to call those experiences into question. Since many of the disciples are fisher-men, they know how bad things can get on open water. Their question at the end of the passage—"Who is this? Even the wind and the waves obey him!"—suggests that their uncertainty about who Jesus is and what he is capable of lies behind fear. But their first question—"Don't you care?"—exposes perhaps the biggest concern: Even if Jesus is someone who can help them, does he care enough to do so? Perhaps the disciples' greatest fear is that God is real and powerful but uncaring. So what about us? Why are we so afraid? What circumstances make us afraid? What beliefs about Jesus or about God do we challenge in our fear?

Continue the Conversation

Jesus: Why are you so afraid?

Me: ....

....

....

....

....

....

....

....

....

....

....

....

....

....

Thursday, Week 3

· · · · · · · · · · · · ·

Read Luke 9:22-25.

"The Son of Man must suffer many things and be rejected by the elders, the chief priests and the teachers of the law, and he must be killed and on the third day be raised to life." Then [Jesus] said to them all: "Whoever wants to be my disciple must deny themselves and take up their cross daily and follow me. For whoever wants to save their life will lose it, but whoever loses their life for me will save it. **What good is it for someone to gain the whole world, and yet lose or forfeit their very self?"**

Reflection

In these verses, Jesus hints at the reason why everything in his world always seems to be upside-down: His future consists of dying a brutal death and being raised again. Jesus' life models this inversion of our expectations: "Whoever wants to save their life will lose it, but whoever loses their life for me will save it." (We see this fundamental law restated in other terms in passages like Matthew 20:16: "The last will be first, and the first will be last.") This rule of inversion radically relativizes the value of worldly wealth, power, and prestige and demands that we ask and answer Jesus' question: "What good is it for someone to gain the whole world, and yet lose or forfeit their very self?"

Continue the Conversation

Jesus: What good is it for [you] to gain the whole world, and yet lose or forfeit [your] very self?

Me: ....

....

....

....

....

....

....

....

....

....

....

....

Friday, Week 3

· · · · · · · · · · · ·

Read Mark 6:31-44.

Because so many people were coming and going that they did not even have a chance to eat, [Jesus] said to them, "Come with me by yourselves to a quiet place and get some rest." So they went away by themselves in a boat to a solitary place. But many who saw them leaving recognized them and ran on foot from all the towns and got there ahead of them. When Jesus landed and saw a large crowd, he had compassion on them, because they were like sheep without a shepherd. So he began teaching them many things. By this time it was late in the day, so his disciples came to him. "This is a remote place," they said, "and it's already very late. Send the people away so that they can go to the surrounding countryside and villages and buy themselves something to eat." But he answered, "You give them something to eat." They said to him, "That would take more than half a year's wages! Are we to go and spend that much on bread and give it to them to eat?" **"How many loaves do you have?"** he asked. "Go and see." When they found out, they said, "Five—and two fish." Then Jesus directed them to have all the people sit down in groups on the green grass. So they sat down in groups of hundreds and fifties. Taking the five loaves and the two fish and looking up to heaven, he gave thanks and broke the loaves. Then he gave them to his disciples to distribute to the people. He also divided the two fish among them all. They all ate and were satisfied, and the disciples picked up twelve basketfuls of broken pieces of bread and fish. The number of the men who had eaten was five thousand.

Reflection

Jesus faces an overwhelming problem: thousands of people in the desert with nothing to eat. The disciples go to Jesus with the problem but, shockingly, he turns it back on them: "You give them something to eat." There's no way this group of (now-unemployed) fishermen has enough resources to buy all the food that would be needed. Yet Jesus is undeterred: "How many loaves do you have?" When the disciples check and report back, they witness Jesus miraculously multiplying the little bit they have so that it is enough to feed thousands. The lesson: We shouldn't focus on what we lack but on what we have. Jesus can multiply what we have so that it's enough. And this is just as much true for who we are as it is for what we have. On my own, I may not be up to the task of what God calls me to do, but, with Jesus' help, I have what I need.

Continue the Conversation

Jesus: How many loaves do you have?

Me: ....

....

....

....

....

....

....

....

....

....

....

....

....

Week 4

Does This Offend You?

God has a habit of working in ways that I find annoying. One of my best friends started following Jesus after reading an evangelistic tract, despite the fact that I believe tracts to be impersonal, offensive, and ineffective. And I know an extended family member whose life was transformed through a God-encounter mediated by the recovery of a lost pet. Particularly upsetting to me was the time my small-group leader, a woman whom I trust deeply, experienced a miraculous healing of cold sores after a televangelist encouraged her to place her hands on her television screen. Mere seconds after placing her hands on the screen, she was instantly and verifiably healed. Her husband, whom I also trust, confirms the story. I don't know what's worse: the report of this miraculous, straightforward healing in a season of life during which a friend of mine in his mid-twenties was dying of allegedly treatable cancer or the fact that the healing was facilitated by a televangelist with theology and politics that I found distasteful at best and dangerous at worst. God's total disregard for my cultural, political, and theological preferences is deeply troubling and profoundly offensive to my sense of how God and the world ought to work.

This chapter is centered on a question Jesus asks that many of us may feel the need to answer in the affirmative from time to time: "Does this offend you?"

Jesus asks this question in the midst of a lengthy—and, frankly, pretty offensive—teaching recorded in the Gospel of John. This particular teaching may offend us for any number of reasons, but we will consider two. First, Jesus calls out our insufficiency by insisting on our need for him and saying that he is the only way. Second, he also says he's the only requirement, meaning Jesus will welcome some people we'd rather not see him embrace. So, as we "listen" together, we should consider not only whether or why the folks in the passage are offended by what Jesus has to say but also whether and why we might be offended. If we find the answer to Jesus' question "Does this offend you?" is "Yes," we can say so and expect Jesus to meet us in that answer, encounter us in that offense, and walk together with us from that place.

· · · · · ·

Jesus has just finished performing one of his most famous miracles: feeding more than five thousand people with just a couple loaves of bread and a few small fish. Wanting a break from the crowds, he goes across the lake. But the crowd chases after him. When they find him, Jesus basically tells them that if they're chasing after him because he's able to multiply bread, they're doing the right thing for the wrong reason. This begins a long conversation about bread. The people seem to have an expectation that the Messiah—the anointed future king of Israel—will bring "bread from heaven" like the manna that God miraculously provided for the ancient Israelites. They want to know if Jesus will perform a "bread from heaven" miracle for them.

Jesus then explains that the "true bread from heaven" is himself, which, granted, is difficult to understand. Jesus goes on to say that this bread brings eternal life. These audacious claims elicit some complaints from the crowd. They ask, "Is this not Jesus, the son of Joseph, whose father and mother we know? How can he now say, 'I came down from heaven'?" (John 6:42). They know where he's from—and it's not heaven. Jesus' response only ups the ante; apparently, they don't understand because God hasn't given them the necessary insight. Jesus says, "Everyone who has heard the Father and learned from him comes to me" (John 6:45).

Then, Jesus explains the matter as plainly as he can:

> "Very truly, I tell you, the one who believes has eternal life. I am the bread of life. Your ancestors ate the manna in the wilderness, yet they died. But here is the bread that comes down from heaven, which anyone may eat and not die. I am the living bread that came down from heaven. Whoever eats this bread will live forever. This bread is my flesh, which I will give for the life of the world." Then the Jews began to argue sharply among themselves, "How can this man give us his flesh to eat?" (John 6:47-52)

When the people begin to argue among themselves, wondering how Jesus could give them his flesh to eat, Jesus continues:

> "Very truly I tell you, unless you eat the flesh of the Son of Man and drink his blood, you have no life in you. Whoever eats my flesh and drinks my blood has eternal life, and I will raise them up at the last day. For my flesh is real food and my blood is real drink. Whoever eats my flesh and drinks my blood remains in me, and I in them. Just as the living Father sent me and I live because of the Father, so the one who feeds on me will live because of me. This is the bread that came down from heaven. Your ancestors ate manna and died, but whoever feeds on this bread will live forever." (John 6:53-58)

To get a sense of just how bizarre and offensive Jesus' words are, we have to imagine him pointing at himself while he says the last two lines: "*This* is the bread that came down from heaven. Your ancestors ate manna and died, but whoever feeds on this bread will live forever."

Even Jesus' own disciples are befuddled:

On hearing [Jesus' teaching], many of his disciples said, "This is a
hard teaching. Who can accept it?" Aware that his disciples were
grumbling about this, Jesus said to them, "Does this offend you?
Then what if you see the Son of Man ascend to where he was before!
The Spirit gives life; the flesh counts for nothing. The words I have
spoken to you—they are full of the Spirit and life. . . . This is why I
told you that no one can come to me unless the Father has enabled
them." (John 6:60-63, 65)

"This is a hard teaching," the disciples say—talk about an understatement.
There are multiple offenses here. It's like a cascade of offense, each one leading
to the next. Let's just admit our discomfort: Eating Jesus' flesh and drinking his
blood is an intense, confusing image. It's especially offensive to the religious folks
hearing Jesus' message because eating blood was against the religious law; God had
called it was unlawful. (See Genesis 9:4; Leviticus 17:10-16.) So Jesus' prescription
here is not just intense and weird—it goes against religious law. But that's not the
major problem with Jesus' teaching. The "eating my flesh" part is weird, sure, but
let's look at the central issue: Jesus insists that we all *need* him. He claims that this
intimate dependence is not optional; it's basic to life itself. This claim only deepens
the sense of offensiveness and the vividness of Jesus' metaphor.

In Leviticus, the reason we aren't supposed to eat blood has everything to
do with the idea that blood represents the life of the animal itself. This makes
blood sacred; this gives it its atoning function. So, basically, when Jesus suggests that everyone needs his blood, he is saying, "You're dead. You have no life
within you. You need mine." This is Jesus' assessment of our status without him:
We have no life on our own. That being said, we need to hear what Jesus is *not*
saying: Jesus is *not* saying that we are worthless. This is abundantly clear from
the broader arc of the Bible as a whole. The Bible regularly affirms the goodness of each divine creation and the joy that God takes in God's creation. Right
from the beginning, creation involved not only forming Adam out of the dust
but also breathing Divine life into his newly created body. It wasn't enough to
form us and leave us alone. God put God's breath within us. The goodness God

affirmed in us from the very beginning relates to what Jesus is coming to fulfill. Jesus doesn't say there's nothing of value in us—quite the opposite. He says that there are treasures of God waiting to be unlocked, unleashed, turned on, turned up, and set loose. But they lie dormant, dead, waiting for the breath of God to breathe on them and put them in motion. Who we are fundamentally comes from this divine breath, this divine Spirit, that Jesus says has been sent from heaven in his very person.

We need an intimate relationship with Jesus not unlike the relationship Jesus has with his and our heavenly Father: a relationship of abiding, of dwelling within, as close as our relationship with what we eat. This relationship transgresses the boundaries of our very bodies. As we take Jesus in—eat his flesh, drink his blood, breathe in his Spirit—he becomes part of us. His life becomes our life. Like Adam and Eve in the Garden, the awesome potentialities of human existence—which lie dormant within us—are brought to life by the Life dwelling within.

Ultimately, this is Jesus' message to his disciples and to us: "You're dead. You have no life in you—*unless* you eat my flesh *and* drink my blood." If we do so, unlike in Leviticus, eating Jesus' body and drinking Jesus' blood will be a *good* thing because the life that Jesus has within him is exactly the life we need. We who have no life will then have life—Jesus' life—within us. So, the stakes could not be higher. They are quite literally life and death.

· · · · · ·

In this teaching, Jesus' body becomes bread from heaven—divine provision to us in our time in the desert—and his blood becomes the atoning sacrifice. Moreover, his flesh and his blood become the force of life itself, the breath that calls our dead bodies into life. Jesus is the source of the life we need. Without him, without taking him into our very bodies, we lie dead. With him, we have life—life eternal.

Jesus' words boil down to this: Jesus is the only way. Not only are we *dead* without Jesus, but also only this intimate relationship with Jesus can bring life. And Jesus claims this is a *universal* condition. Unless we eat, we have no life in us. "Everyone who has heard the Father and learned from him comes to me," he says. That is, if we don't come to Jesus, we don't know God. Jesus finally states it plainly in John 14:6: "I am the way and the truth and the life. No one comes to the Father except through me." If we ranked all Jesus' teachings in order of their popularity in our culture—from his most popular, "Do not judge lest you be judged" through his other greatest hits, such as, "Love your neighbor as yourself" and "Blessed are the poor," all the way down to his most offensive, this statement would be at the very bottom. It's just so absolute, so exclusive. In a world full of diversity and differences, how can Jesus say that all people—no matter their culture, gender, sexuality, identity, past, or present—need the same thing: him? It's outrageous.

Does this offend you?

· · · · · ·

For some, the scandal of Jesus' words is that Jesus is the only *way*; for others, the scandal is that Jesus is the only *requirement*. This second idea can be especially troubling for lifelong Christians who have bought into the idea that they have cornered the market on spiritual knowledge. A pernicious sort of ego loves the idea that the whole world needs what only "we" have. But, of course, the idea that we *possess* Jesus—when, in fact, it is he who supplies our very life—is ridiculous. What Jesus gives us, we receive only as a gift; what we possess as religious people is just the trappings: our culture, our practices, our ethics, and the like. In insisting that *he*—and only he—is what the world needs, Jesus suggests that these cultural trappings aren't as important as we thought. And this statement offends his audience because it transgresses their cultural and religious boundaries. As he tells them that their festival celebrating the miraculous provision in the desert is now being fulfilled by the divine sustenance made available in his own body, as he invites them to imagine doing something that goes against their religious law, Jesus offends his ancient audience. And we may be offended too if we're caught up in our own privilege at having "gotten it right." Because if Jesus is the only requirement, then while everyone may need Jesus, not everyone needs my culture, my ethics, or even my *religion*.

I've experienced this offense time and again in my life whenever I've strayed into that smug religious self-satisfaction. As surely as Jesus shows himself sufficient in transgressing various cultural boundaries, my cultural categories show themselves to be mere religious window dressing. Hannah and I experienced this in striking ways during the summer we spent studying in Ghana. As we spent time with followers of Jesus with radically different cultural practices than our own, folks who depended on God's provision in such a visceral way that it struck me as superstition, people who encountered Jesus in the traditional religious practices of the local shrines—including animal sacrifice—it didn't take long for me to realize that these people didn't need my culture. They didn't even want my learned post-colonial assessment of their lack of desire for my culture. They had Jesus; they had life. As a result, I was unnecessary, save as a fellow follower on the journey of life with Jesus. Experiences like this helpfully offend my sense of religio-cultural pride and expose it as the arrogance it is.

A few years ago, a friend forwarded me a music video for the song "Jesus" by Mo Sabri. Sabri is a Muslim, yet his song is all about this central orientation of his life around the life and teachings of Jesus. And he gets quite a few things *right* about Jesus. He identifies the centrality of following Jesus, of taking on Jesus' life and being transformed in the process, of living a life marked by encounters with Jesus, and of being transformed by Jesus' simple principles of love. His focus on how his devotion shapes his way of life more than a mere confession of faith is something from which many Christians—including myself—could learn quite a bit. His conviction that following Jesus requires doing what Jesus says is, frankly, deeply biblical. (See John 15:14.) Again, Mo Sabri is a Muslim; he's not a Christian, and he's not interested in *becoming* a Christian. Still, he seems to be following Jesus. I mean, what do I know? I'm pretty sure he and I would disagree about any number of theological points, but Jesus' life seems to be in him.

If we're offended—either by the idea that Jesus is the only way or by the idea that Jesus is the only requirement—I believe Jesus would offer us this diagnosis: "You're offended because you still think you have what it takes for your own life, for the lives of others around you. You think you have what it takes—individually or as part of a religious group or culture—but apart from me, there is no life in you. And that offends your sense of self-sufficiency, your sense of pride."

· · · · · ·

One summer when I was in college, I interned at a church of more than ten thousand people in the suburbs of Chicago. The church's campus was enormous and built around a lake. I was a music intern with the young adults' ministry, playing in one of the bands, writing some music, producing some video material for services, pitching in here and there on the creative team. One evening after a Saturday night service, as I was driving home, I sensed an invitation to stop and sit by the lake. It had been a hard summer. At the beginning of my internship, I had broken my finger and was only so useful as a pianist. I had also begun losing hearing in one of my ears, further decreasing my utility. I was experiencing viscerally Jesus' diagnosis that "the flesh is useless." Increasingly, I was feeling like a small fish in a ten-thousand-person pond, wondering who I was and what my purpose was.

As I sat beside the lake that night, I asked God why I was brought to this internship if only to waste my last summer of college. I wasn't getting paid—in fact, I was spending a good deal of money on gas for the hour-long commute each way from my parents' house. "What is this all for?" I asked. "Why did you bring me here?" And I remember God speaking to me in that moment—not in words, exactly, but with great clarity nonetheless: "Matt, do you feel this weakness? This dependence? Do you feel what it's like to come to the end of yourself and experience this need that you have for me? That's what this summer is for. You need to know what it is to need me, and you need to come to terms with it. Running on the illusion of your own sufficiency isn't going to get you very far. If you want to follow Jesus, you have to come to terms with your needs. And you have to learn to trust that while you don't have what it takes, I do. And if you learn that this summer, it will be the best internship you ever have." Indeed, that summer was full of God's provision for me, meeting me in my weakness, teaching me to lean on God's presence, to take God in, to breathe in God's Spirit—for

Jesus himself to be my sustenance when my former diet of accolades and pride dried up, leaving me empty.

I returned to school that fall, and folks asked me how my summer was. "It was awesome," I replied. "I was useless. I accomplished almost nothing. Willow Creek Community Church will never remember my presence there. But I think I've started to figure out something about this following Jesus thing. I know more than ever that I need him, and his life within me is worth all the rest."

· · · · · ·

Jesus' primary offense is that he says we need him, that apart from him, there is no life in us. And the danger—the reason Jesus asks us this question point-blank—is this: If we get snagged on this offense, we may never experience the life Jesus offers. Would we be so offended by a chef's diagnosis of our hunger, for example, that we would refuse the banquet he offers? "Why are you offering me all this food—are you calling me hungry?!" That would be ridiculous. The danger is that the offense of Jesus' diagnosis of our need may blind us to the abundance that he invites us to receive, and that would be quite a loss. Indignant at the naming of our hunger, we'll starve. Offended by the diagnosis of our disease, we'll waste away. We need to see the offense for what it is: a simple statement of truth. Then, we can come to the table to eat of the banquet that Jesus has prepared for us and be transformed as his life takes up residence within us. We'll get to celebrate the abundant life that he makes available for us, free of offense, free of the desire to hide our needs, free to be overjoyed at the goodness of creation formed, breathed, and redeemed in us.

Monday, Week 4

· · · · · · · · · · · ·

Read John 6:53-61.

Jesus said to them, "Very truly I tell you, unless you eat the flesh of the Son of Man and drink his blood, you have no life in you. Whoever eats my flesh and drinks my blood has eternal life, and I will raise them up at the last day. For my flesh is real food and my blood is real drink. Whoever eats my flesh and drinks my blood remains in me, and I in them. Just as the living Father sent me and I live because of the Father, so the one who feeds on me will live because of me. This is the bread that came down from heaven. Your ancestors ate manna and died, but whoever feeds on this bread will live forever." He said this while teaching in the synagogue in Capernaum. On hearing it, many of his disciples said, "This is a hard teaching. Who can accept it?" Aware that his disciples were grumbling about this, Jesus said to them, **"Does this offend you?"**

Reflection

Picture Jesus pointing at his body as he says, "Whoever feeds on *this* bread will live forever." It's not hard to imagine how this metaphor tripped up more than a few people. (Indeed, in the ancient world, Christians were regularly mocked as cannibals because they talked about consuming the body and blood of Jesus in their worship meetings.) But perhaps the meaning of the metaphor is even more offensive than the metaphor itself. In this passage, Jesus claims that his very self is the sustenance we're looking for, that, even though we may chase after many things in our lives, we only need one thing: him. In our world, this is perhaps the most offensive claim Jesus makes: he—and only he—is what everyone needs. Many of us don't like to think of ourselves as having needs. And if we concede that we have needs, we imagine that we're unique enough that no one-size-fits-all solution exists. Still, Jesus says that he is the source of life for all. Does this offend you?

Continue the Conversation

Jesus: Does this offend you?

Me: ....

....

....

....

....

....

....

....

....

....

....

....

....

....

Tuesday, Week 4

. . . .

Read John 6:66-69.

From this time many of his disciples turned back and no longer followed him. **"You do not want to leave too, do you?"** Jesus asked the Twelve. Simon Peter answered him, "Lord, to whom shall we go? You have the words of eternal life. We have come to believe and to know that you are the Holy One of God."

Reflection

Jesus' offense (see previous daily reflection) is apparently great enough that many decide to stop following him rather than struggle with the offense. Enough are walking away that Jesus turns and addresses his twelve closest followers, his twelve best friends: "You do not want to leave too, do you?" Jesus' exclusive claims may seem drastic enough to make us want to walk away. Why does he have to claim to be the only way? Jesus' question, then, is for us too. Jesus wants to know if following him is too costly. If this is Jesus' question to us, perhaps we can take heart from Peter's answer: "To whom shall we go? You have the words of eternal life."

Time and again, for various reasons, walking away from Jesus has seemed like an attractive option to me. But instead of turning away, I end up responding much like Peter: "I've seen and experienced too much. I've seen God answer prayer. I've seen people healed. I've known a love and a calming presence too great for words. Where else can I go? Following Jesus is the only way for me." Still, this response isn't true for everyone. No matter where we find ourselves in our desire to follow Jesus, answering Jesus' question may help us discover what we have to anchor ourselves through the inevitable storms of worry, fear, doubt, and offense.

Continue the Conversation

Jesus: You do not want to leave too, do you?

Me: ....

....

....

....

....

....

....

....

....

....

....

....

....

....

Wednesday, Week 4

. . . .

Read Luke 6:46-49.

"Why do you call me, 'Lord, Lord,' and do not do what I say? As for everyone who comes to me and hears my words and puts them into practice, I will show you what they are like. They are like a man building a house, who dug down deep and laid the foundation on rock. When a flood came, the torrent struck that house but could not shake it, because it was well built. But the one who hears my words and does not put them into practice is like a man who built a house on the ground without a foundation. The moment the torrent struck that house, it collapsed and its destruction was complete."

Reflection

Jesus isn't looking for flatterers; he's looking for followers. He's not looking for people to call him *Lord*; he's looking for people to treat him as Lord. Apparently, this is for our own good. Jesus says that building our lives on obedience is like building a house on a firm foundation. When the floods come, the house stands firm. A life built on obedience to Jesus can withstand opposition—whether worry, fear, doubt, or offense. Nevertheless, obedience is difficult, so Jesus' question is worth pondering. Why don't we do what he says? Is it because Jesus' words are difficult to put into practice? Is it because Jesus' way is costly—in terms of time, money, and reputation? What entices us to build our lives on an unsure foundation?

Continue the Conversation

Jesus: Why do you call me, "Lord, Lord," and do not do what I say?

Me: ....

....

....

....

....

....

....

....

....

....

....

....

....

....

Thursday, Week 4

. . . .

Read John 9:1, 6-7, 13-17, 24-25, 34-38.

As [Jesus] went along, he saw a man blind from birth. . . . [Jesus] spit on the ground, made some mud with the saliva, and put it on the man's eyes. "Go," he told him, "wash in the Pool of Siloam" (this word means "Sent"). So the man went and washed, and came home seeing. . . . They brought to the Pharisees the man who had been blind. Now the day on which Jesus had made the mud and opened the man's eyes was a Sabbath. Therefore the Pharisees also asked him how he had received his sight. "He put mud on my eyes," the man replied, "and I washed, and now I see." Some of the Pharisees said, "This man is not from God, for he does not keep the Sabbath." But others asked, "How can a sinner perform such signs?" So they were divided. Then they turned again to the blind man, "What have you to say about him? It was your eyes he opened." The man replied, "He is a prophet." . . . A second time [the Pharisees] summoned the man who had been blind. "Give glory to God by telling the truth," they said. "We know this man is a sinner." He replied, "Whether he is a sinner or not, I don't know. One thing I do know. I was blind but now I see!" . . . And they threw him out. Jesus heard that they had thrown him out, and when he found him, he said, **"Do you believe in the Son of Man?"** "Who is he, sir?" the man asked. "Tell me so that I may believe in him." Jesus said, "You have now seen him; in fact, he is the one speaking with you." Then the man said, "Lord, I believe," and he worshiped him.

Reflection

The story begins with an amazing feat: A man born blind can see after his encounter with Jesus. But things go awry, and the blind man finds himself caught in a conversation about Jesus offering healing on the sabbath, which religious law decrees as a day of rest, and whether that makes Jesus a sinner. Sadly, this is sometimes how it goes for us: A genuine encounter with Jesus gets lost in a tangle of questions from others that totally miss the point. Though the formerly blind man tries to explain the obvious—"Whether he is a sinner or not, I don't know. One thing I do know. I was blind but now I see!"—the Pharisees will not listen. When Jesus hears about the Pharisees' questioning, he asks the question that does matter: "Do you believe in the Son of Man?"

Continue the Conversation

Jesus: Do you believe [*or* trust] in the Son of Man?

Me: ....

....

....

....

....

....

....

....

....

....

....

....

....

....

Friday, Week 4

. . . .

Read John 13:31-38.

Jesus said, "Now the Son of Man is glorified and God is glorified in him. If God is glorified in him, God will glorify the Son in himself, and will glorify him at once. My children, I will be with you only a little longer. You will look for me, and just as I told the Jews, so I tell you now: Where I am going, you cannot come. A new command I give you: Love one another. As I have loved you, so you must love one another. By this everyone will know that you are my disciples, if you love one another." Simon Peter asked him, "Lord, where are you going?" Jesus replied, "Where I am going, you cannot follow now, but you will follow later." Peter asked, "Lord, why can't I follow you now? I will lay down my life for you." Then Jesus answered, "**Will you really lay down your life for me?** Very truly I tell you, before the rooster crows, you will disown me three times!"

Reflection

The mystery of Jesus' glory is about to be revealed. Jesus is going to the cross. But before he goes, Jesus gives a new commandment to his disciples: He commands them to love one another the same way that he loves them. What exactly this looks like, they don't know. Jesus has offered hints along the way that perhaps following him would cost the disciples' lives (see Luke 9:23-24), but, for now, the disciples are focused on Jesus' departure. "Why can't I follow you now?" Peter asks. If Peter has learned anything in his life with Jesus, he knows that where Jesus goes, he ought to follow. Yet, at what seems to be a crucial moment in Jesus' ministry, the disciples cannot follow him. Desperate to prove his allegiance, Peter promises, "I will lay down my life for you." Jesus looks him straight in the eye and asks, "Will you really lay down your life for me?" It can be easy for us to think we're ready to make a whole-life commitment before we really are. Some parts of our lives can seem relatively easy to lay down; other parts are much more difficult. So we must ask ourselves, *What is Jesus inviting me to lay down for his sake? What am I still holding back?*

Continue the Conversation

Jesus: Will you really lay down your life for me?

Me: ....

....

....

....

....

....

....

....

....

....

....

....

....

Who Do You Say
I Am?

My faith nearly didn't survive seminary. Sometimes people assume that seminary is a time of incredible faith-building. Studying the Bible, theology, the history of God's people—how could that be anything but faith-forming? And, in part, it was. But, overall, I would describe seminary as part of a great disillusionment in my life. Crazier still, it felt like no one bore more responsibility for that disillusionment than *God*. I used to tell people that sometimes I felt as though God was causing me to lose my faith.

Some of my challenges were pretty typical, almost predictable. Studying the history of *anything* introduces us to new ideas, contradictions, and questions we haven't dealt with before. As I became more familiar with the composition of the Bible and the various cultures to which it was addressed, it stopped being this magic book that could only tell the truth. And that was hard to deal with. At the same time, I started to realize just how much of my theology—my ideas *about* God—were the result of culture: white culture, European culture, imperialistic culture. I began to wonder what of all I thought I knew about "God" was *really* God? These were profound challenges; my fundamental conceptions about God began to shift. Throughout the process, I heard Jesus asking me again and again—with an urgency that hadn't been present for some time—"Who do you say I am?"

In this chapter, we arrive at perhaps the single most important question Jesus asks in the Gospels, the one on which all the others depend, the one upon which the orientation of our lives depends. As high as the stakes are here, we may have a sneaking suspicion that this is where Jesus is less interested in an honest answer than in the "right" answer. Yet, even—or especially—when it comes to this central question, Jesus most wants a genuine *conversation* about who we've come to know Jesus to be and who he is in our lives.

· · · · · ·

This question appears in a passage that begins, like so many other important moments between Jesus and his disciples, on the road:

> Jesus and his disciples went on to the villages around Caesarea Philippi. On the way he asked them, "Who do people say I am?" They replied, "Some say John the Baptist; others say Elijah; and still others, one of the prophets." "But what about you?" he asked. "Who do you say I am?" Peter answered, "You are the Messiah." Jesus warned them not to tell anyone about him. He then began to teach them that the Son of Man must suffer many things and be rejected by the elders, the chief priests and the teachers of the law, and that he must be killed and after three days rise again. He spoke plainly about this, and Peter took him aside and began to rebuke him. But when Jesus turned and looked at his disciples, he rebuked Peter. "Get behind me, Satan!" he said. "You do not have in mind the concerns of God, but merely human concerns." Then he called the crowd to him along with his disciples and said: "Whoever wants to be my disciple must deny themselves and take up their cross and follow me. For whoever wants to save their life will lose it, but whoever loses their life for me and for the gospel will save it. (Mark 8:27-35)

Before Jesus gets to his main question, he asks a sort of warm-up question: "Who do people say I am?" Ultimately, Jesus wants to know what his disciples think, but he starts by asking them to assess the general public's sentiment. After all, more often than not, what we think about Jesus depends, to some degree, on what others have said. Our beliefs are shaped by what we've heard from our families or friends or religious communities. We're influenced by what we read in the news or on social media or see on television. Our understanding of Jesus is inevitably intertwined with others' understandings of Jesus, so Jesus wants to know, "Who do people say I am?" The disciples answer, "Some say John the Baptist; others say Elijah; and still others, one of the prophets." The people are all suggesting, one way or another, that Jesus basically fits into a category with which they're familiar. John the Baptist had recently made a big splash as a religious teacher; Elijah was a great hero of old. Perhaps one of these characters holds the key to understanding who Jesus is. Or maybe Jesus fits better in the broader category of *prophet*.

How often do we do the same thing? We place Jesus into a preexisting category, a neat box tied in a bow. Perhaps we think of Jesus as a political hero—a head of state or a patriot. Or perhaps we think of Jesus as an activist or a radical, like Martin Luther King Jr., Che Guevara, or Angela Davis. Certainly, there's a stream of thinking that sees Jesus as Tony Robbins: a motivational coach who can unlock our inner potential. Or perhaps he's someone whose goal is to help us better understand ourselves, like Oprah or a good therapist. For some, maybe the best comparison would be Elon Musk or Steve Jobs, wonder-workers in their own right. Like these modern masters of technology, Jesus too can supply us with the means to achieve our dreams.

And what about more religious comparisons? Perhaps we think of Jesus as a religious teacher—a wise man, someone who has all the answers. Or we imagine Jesus as King of the cosmos, a puppet master behind the scenes, pulling the strings to make everything happen. Maybe we've heard Jesus described as the ultimate judge of a world he would rather do without. Along these lines, some see Jesus as a bigot and, therefore, the quintessential hypocrite: judgmental Jesus who taught others not to judge. Others see Jesus as the founder and champion of

Christianity—the captain of "Team Christian," who leads the charge in a competition among other world religions. And what about Jesus as our best friend—someone who validates everything we do and just wants to be our buddy? We ought to think seriously and critically about how these cultural lenses affect how we understand Jesus. They're not neutral. Even if and when they capture something right about Jesus, they distort something else. As we'll see, every answer to this question does exactly that.

Initially, Jesus wants to know what's being said *out there* about him, what the opinion polls are reporting. Ultimately, however, Jesus wants to know who we say he is. He wants to know what we think. Jesus' fundamental question to us isn't "How does your culture see me?", "Who does that author say I am?", "Who does that pastor say I am?", "Who does the church say I am?", or even "Who does the Bible say I am?" Any number of those answers might be revelatory in some way or another. Those answers can be helpful, maybe even essential to the process of working out our own answers (the Bible could be described that way). But the question Jesus has for us is this: "Who do *you* say I am?" That is, "What do you think? What's your take? Not because it's better or more informed or even necessarily 'right,' but because it's *your* answer." Regardless of what other people say and who Jesus *actually* is, what matters most for our lives is who he is *for us*. Jesus may be God. He may be Truth in the form of a person. But if he's not that *for us*, then what does that have to do with our lives? And Jesus is interested in our lives.

Jesus' question, persistently, in every moment, in every interaction is this: "What about *you*, who do *you* say I am?" This question is concealed just below the surface of every other question Jesus asks. "What do you want me to do for you?" leads to "Do you believe that I am trustworthy with your hearts deepest desires?" "Has no one condemned you?" leads to "Do you believe *I* will condemn you?" "Why do you worry?" leads to "Do you believe I am trustworthy?" "Does this offend you?" is basically "Am *I* offensive to you?" Ultimately, they all lead to "Who do you say I am?" Not because Jesus is needy and requires our affirmation—nor because he needs our help figuring out who he is. Jesus knows who he is in terms of his identity as God's beloved. No, Jesus is so persistent because this question—who we say Jesus is—is the most important question of our lives. Everything depends on it. It can sound crazy, this idea that our take on the identity of a guy who lived in Palestine some two thousand years ago is somehow the key to life. But I really think it's the case. And so it is for our sake—not for his—that Jesus asks us again and again, patiently but persistently, "Who do you say I am?"

· · · · · ·

When Jesus presents the disciples with a question—perhaps, *the* question—we may be able to guess who's going to venture an answer if we have any experience with the Gospels: Peter. And Peter does indeed answer, saying, "You are the Messiah" (Mark 8:29). That's a potent answer, though perhaps one that's become a bit obscure to us. Perhaps *Messiah* has become one of those generic religious words that doesn't mean much. This would not have been the case for Peter or for the rest of the disciples. When Peter says, "You are the Messiah," he's naming Jesus as the lynchpin of the history of God's people, the person upon whom the whole history of Israel rests. The word *Messiah* means the "anointed one," the one appointed to be king. If others describe Jesus as a prophet of one kind or another, Peter describes Jesus as a *king*—or at least a king in waiting, someone on his way to becoming king. If others describe Jesus as *Elijah*, the great prophet of the people of God, Peter suggests that Jesus is *David*, the great king. Like David, Jesus was *anointed* years before he came into his kingdom, before he was enthroned. Calling Jesus "the anointed one" suggests that Jesus is a royal figure and also explains, by way of reference to the story of David, how it is that he might not yet be recognized universally as king. *Messiah* explains how Jesus could be king but not yet be recognized as such.

Apparently, Peter gets the question right. In the Gospel of Mark, there's no clearer sign that someone has insight into who Jesus is than when Jesus sternly orders them not to tell anyone about his identity. (See Mark 8:30.) Peter has given the right answer. No doubt about it. What's surprising, though, is where that right answer leads. After Jesus begins to teach the disciples that he will suffer and die, "Peter took him aside and began to rebuke him" (Mark 8:32). It's one of the most stunning moments in the Gospels: Peter *rebukes* the man he just proclaimed as the Messiah. Jesus faces plenty of opposition during his ministry: from the scribes, the Pharisees, the Romans. But none of them has the gall to pull Jesus aside and lecture him on how to do his job. Even Judas has the good sense to betray Jesus under the cover of darkness.

Jesus' response is swift and surgical: "When Jesus turned and looked at his disciples, he rebuked Peter. 'Get behind me, Satan!' he said. 'You do not have in mind the concerns of God, but merely human concerns'" (Mark 8:33). Peter has clearly screwed up here, as Jesus' response shows us. Peter's rebuke has revealed a serious mistake about the way Peter—who just gave the "right" answer—sees Jesus. From the response that Jesus gives, we can reconstruct the content of Peter's rebuke and, indeed, it seems that Peter's rebuke of Jesus is rooted precisely in his "correct" answer about Jesus' identity. It's all about what the word *Messiah* means—to Peter and to Jesus. When Peter says that Jesus is Messiah, he means monarch-in-waiting, political revolutionary about to begin the uprising. When Peter says that Jesus is the Messiah, he is imagining precisely the opposite of suffering, rejection, and death. In fairness to Peter, the title may have meant something similar to a lot of folks in Judaea in those days.

When Jesus, having affirmed Peter's identification of him as the Messiah, launches into this description of his coming crucifixion, Peter feels emboldened to correct Jesus based on the "right answer" he has given already: "You can't suffer and die; you're the Messiah, the anointed one." That's when Peter becomes Satan—the accuser, the tempter, the one potentially leading Jesus and, more importantly, the other disciples astray. Jesus has to rebuke Peter in front of the other disciples. All of this happens because Peter thought he knew who Jesus was because he gave the right answer. Claiming to know Jesus' identity is a dangerous move in the Gospel of Mark. The only people who say they know who Jesus is in Mark are demons, Peter (right before being called *Satan*), and the centurion who kills Jesus. This is not good company.

There's something for us to learn here, especially from the responses of the characters whom the Gospel holds up as examples: the wondering of the disciples (see Mark 4:41); the townspeople who can't dare to speak their confessions as more than questions (see Mark 6:2); the fear and awe of the women at the tomb that drives them to reverent silence (see Mark 16:8). We should learn to imitate their first instinct: to linger for a moment in Jesus' ineffable presence, to revel in what we experience of Jesus that can't be put into words, to state our hunches about Jesus in questions rather than answers, as cries of worshipful wonder rather than theological doctrines or philosophical propositions. In fact, we may be tempted never to dare say who Jesus is or only to respond in pious silence. But that can't be right; the New Testament is full of people whom God blesses as they boldly proclaim who they've come to know Jesus to be.

Given the importance of this bold proclamation, perhaps Peter is our model after all. That is, we need *both* to dare to say who we've come to know Jesus to be *and* to be prepared to receive the inevitable correction that comes from Jesus when our answers lead us astray. In other words, we need to be in relationship—in dialogue—with Jesus. The goal is not to get the "right answer." Or perhaps the "right answer" is simply to remain in conversation with Jesus, to stick around after class, to know that our language doesn't tell the whole story. And, when our language does fail, to allow Jesus to correct us.

Demonic knowledge is stubborn knowledge. "Knowledge puffs up while love builds up" (1 Cor. 8:1). Jesus doesn't want us to have knowledge *about* him. He wants us to have knowledge *of* him, to love him. Better to be a fool enraptured with Jesus than someone with all the "right" answers who's long been done with him. Knowing the right answer isn't the end but rather the beginning of knowing Jesus. In fact, as much as Jesus' identity is the fundamental mystery of the book of Mark, the Gospel begins in a strange way, announcing right from the start that it is "the beginning of the good news about Jesus the Messiah" (1:1). The "right" answer is there from the start, but it's only the beginning of the Gospel's quest to discover who Jesus really is.

We need to know how to use our feeble language to identify Jesus. It's never going to be perfect, but it's all we've got, so we need to learn to use it to make these halting claims about who we know him to be. Twentieth-century German theologian Karl Barth said that we need to be careful about how we use language in talking about God. When we call God *Father*, Barth says, we learn nothing about God but everything about what it means to be a father. For Barth, we don't call God *Father* in order to describe God; we call God *Father* in order to describe how a father ought to be. Now, that might be a bit too extreme to apply strictly in the way we actually use language. But the general point is helpful: Jesus is not like other "objects" we describe with language. When we use language to describe Jesus, our language is transformed. Jesus isn't an empty vessel waiting to be filled with the content of our language. Rather, in comparison to the robust self-defining personal presence that is Jesus, our language is rather like an empty vessel waiting to be filled with the content of who Jesus is. We may attempt to "fill Jesus up" with the content of our language, but the meaning of our words flow "backward," as our words are overwhelmed by the powerful self-revelation of Jesus.

The centurion who witnesses Jesus' death has his language transformed in just this way. When he calls Jesus "Son of God" (see Mark 15:39), he's trying to describe the glory and honor of what he sees before him. (*Son of God* would have been a term he would most naturally have associated with the Emperor.) But this glory and honor—the glory and honor of a man dying naked on a cross, abandoned by his friends—radically transforms what has counted as *glory* and *honor* for him thus far in his life. What begins as a description ends as an epiphany.

We're closest to knowing who Jesus is when we let him inhabit and then break through our cultural boxes. So, maybe Jesus *should* be our political hero. But that should tell us at least as much about political heroes—and about the value of political power—as it tells us about Jesus. Maybe Jesus *should* be our spiritual guru. But that should transform our sense of what it means to come to know ourselves—and even question whether what we really need is simply to come to deeper self-awareness. Perhaps Jesus *should* be the source of our capacity, our strength. But that means thinking about capacity differently than the way we think about tech products that we can use for whatever purpose we choose. God's power doesn't work that way; God's power goes hand in hand with God's will rather than our will.

· · · · · ·

A few years after I finished seminary, while still sorting through the reconfiguration of my faith, a childhood friend of mine and I had a serious email exchange about faith. He's not a follower of Jesus, but he's always been intrigued by faith. He's unconvinced that being good has anything to do with God, but he's genuinely invested in *being good*. He is able to assess himself honestly, understanding that being good doesn't happen by accident or by "being true to oneself." And so, as we were going back and forth in this exchange, he readily agreed that we need something outside ourselves to help us figure out how to "be good," how to do right by ourselves and others. When it came to naming that "something," he couldn't shake this question: Why talk about *Jesus* when we can talk about *love* or *goodness* instead? Perhaps the hardest thing to get on board with about Christianity is the particularity of Jesus, the thought, with which I began the chapter, that somehow life hinges on this Palestinian mystic who walked the world two thousand years ago. If we could get what we wanted of Jesus' goodness without, you know, *Jesus*—if we could abstract Jesus into a principle we could all get on board with, like goodness or love—he would be easier to swallow. I remember my friend sort of suggesting this to me as a potential "product improvement" for my Christianity: I'd have more "takers," he suggested, if I stopped making it all about *Jesus*.

Why not orient our lives around *love*? I mean, the Bible says, "God is love." Why not, as my friend suggested, "do the algebraic substitution" and simplify things? It was a good question that required some serious wrestling. I knew I wasn't tempted to make the trade, but it wasn't immediately clear *why*. As I thought and prayed about the question, a few things occurred to me. First, I'm not sure I'd know what love looks like apart from Jesus. Apart from the Gospel story of Jesus' self-giving love on the cross, I'm not sure I'd get "love" in the abstract right. Second, there's something crucial about the fact that Jesus is a person. Especially if Jesus is one with whom we can be in conversation, then Jesus is so much better than even the best abstract principle. "Love" can't defend itself if we get it completely wrong. Think of the way that some of our best ideas—our best words—have been abused to the point of being used to mean their opposites. *Freedom* becomes grounds for enslaving others. *Peace* becomes the grounds for war. *Truth*—well, I don't even know what to say about what this word has become. No idea can defend itself against our perversion of it. But if we aim not at love in the abstract but at following Jesus, Jesus can correct us. Jesus is love we can consult for clarification. Jesus is goodness in dialogue.

Indeed, over the last dozen years or so, I have come to depend more and more on Jesus but with less and less certainty about the suitability of particular answers to the question: "Who do you say I am?" The hymn that got me through seminary was "My Hope Is Built on Nothing Less." I remember God speaking to me through the words of this old hymn: "On Christ the solid rock I stand / All other ground is sinking sand." On Christ the solid rock I stand—on Jesus, the person whom I know, who knows me, who loves me. He's my rock. And, in comparison, all assumptions, all cultural biases, all politics, all traditions, all ethics, all doctrines, and all religions—*all else* is shifting sand. This song was profoundly orienting, profoundly grounding.

Increasingly, I've come to identify with the observation a mentor of mine shared with me years ago. She said, "You know, the more I follow God, the longer I'm at this whole thing, I find that I have ever more and more questions but also more and more assurance." Assurance—not certainty. Certainty is about what we know in ourselves. It's knowledge we possess; we hold it in our hands. Certainty is about knowledge that puffs up. Assurance is different. Assurance is something we can't have on our own. Assurance is given to us by someone else; it's about relationship. Assurance is standing somewhere firmly but not rigidly. Assurance is a matter of saying, "Here I stand until the One who has placed me here leads me forward."

· · · · · ·

Peter got it backward.

If we have what we're pretty sure is a "right answer" about who Jesus is and then Jesus does something that seems incompatible with that answer, our response should be to let Jesus transform our understanding of what we thought was correct—*not* correct Jesus' behavior to make it fit what we think we know.

When the Bible depicts Jesus spending time with sinners, our response oughtn't be to change the text to make it conform to our sense of what it means that Jesus is "holy" and "without sin." Rather, we should take a step back and reconsider what *holy* means, how Jesus' holiness is one that is able to draw near to sin and not be infected by it but rather overcome it with love. We ought to consider the extent to which the sin that menaces our lives is precisely the sin that makes other sinners untouchable to us. When Jesus shows little concern for religious boundaries—as happy to meet and converse with Samaritans and Gentiles as with Jews—our response shouldn't be to construct new religious boundaries and make Jesus strictly observe them in our world. Rather, we should figure out what it truly means to be "Christian"—to be little Christs. (After all, originally, *Christian* is a noun; it's a person. When we start using *Christian* as an adjective that describes things or institutions or political platforms or celebrities or diets, more often than not, we lose our way.)

Answering Jesus' question—"Who do you say I am?"—means committing to a life in dialogue with him, a life in which Jesus gets to correct our answers, redefine our language, reform our thoughts, and reconnect us to those around us. Through this one question, Jesus can remake our entire world.

Monday, Week 5

. . . .

Read Mark 8:27-35.

Jesus and his disciples went on to the villages around Caesarea Philippi. On the way he asked them, "Who do people say I am?" They replied, "Some say John the Baptist; others say Elijah; and still others, one of the prophets." "But what about you?" he asked. **"Who do you say I am?"** Peter answered, "You are the Messiah." Jesus warned them not to tell anyone about him. He then began to teach them that the Son of Man must suffer many things and be rejected by the elders, the chief priests and the teachers of the law, and that he must be killed and after three days rise again. He spoke plainly about this, and Peter took him aside and began to rebuke him. But when Jesus turned and looked at his disciples, he rebuked Peter. "Get behind me, Satan!" he said. "You do not have in mind the concerns of God, but merely human concerns." Then he called the crowd to him along with his disciples and said: "Whoever wants to be my disciple must deny themselves and take up their cross and follow me. For whoever wants to save their life will lose it, but whoever loses their life for me and for the gospel will save it."

Reflection

"What about you? . . . Who do you say I am?" This is perhaps the most important question Jesus ever asks his disciples. This question drives at the great mystery of the Gospel of Mark: Who is Jesus? Everyone seems to have a different answer to this question, but Jesus wants to know directly from his disciples. Jesus isn't looking necessarily for the "right" answer. In fact, Peter's answer is perfectly "correct." Jesus is the Messiah—that is, the anointed one, the coming King in the kingdom of God. But Jesus tells him not to spread that around, and, immediately following Peter's confession, we see why: As long as Peter is invested in a mistaken understanding of power and authority, labeling Jesus as Messiah—as King—will lead him in the wrong direction, causing him to rebuke Jesus and tell him not to lay down his life.

It's not a quiz; it's not a test. It's an honest question: Who do we say Jesus is? We've encountered Jesus through scripture and conversation for the past few weeks. What have we learned? What have we come to believe about him?

Continue the Conversation

Jesus: Who do you say I am?

Me: You are the Christ. You are my savior and Lord. You saved me from my sins. I am so sorry for not thinking this all the time. I want to follow you forever.

Tuesday, Week 5

· · · · · · · · · · · ·

Read John 18:28-31, 33-37.

[Jesus has been betrayed by one of his disciples and arrested by the religious authorities.]

The Jewish leaders took Jesus from Caiaphas to the palace of the Roman governor . . . Pilate came out to them and asked, "What charges are you bringing against this man?" "If he were not a criminal," they replied, "we would not have handed him over to you." Pilate said, "Take him yourselves and judge him by your own law." "But we have no right to execute anyone," they objected. . . . Pilate then went back inside the palace, summoned Jesus and asked him, "Are you the king of the Jews?" **"Is that your own idea,"** Jesus asked, **"or did others talk to you about me?"** "Am I a Jew?" Pilate replied. "Your own people and chief priests handed you over to me. What is it you have done?" Jesus said, "My kingdom is not of this world. If it were, my servants would fight to prevent my arrest by the Jewish leaders. But now my kingdom is from another place." "You are a king, then!" said Pilate. Jesus answered, "You say that I am a king. In fact, the reason I was born and came into the world is to testify to the truth. Everyone on the side of truth listens to me."

Reflection

Because of Jesus' identification as Messiah, he faces charges of treason against the Roman state. The Roman governor, Pilate, who is not a Jew, doesn't know what to make of the bizarre religious terms used to describe Jesus: *Messiah* and *Christ*. But Jesus avoids using this language to describe himself and has asked others not to use it. So, when Pilate asks him, "Are you the king of the Jews?" Jesus wants to know where this question comes from. The religious authorities' testimony deliberately misleads Pilate; they want him to conclude that Jesus is guilty of treason. But Jesus insists that his kingdom is not earthly; that's why he didn't resist arrest. His kingdom follows divine rather than human logic. Since Jesus is not seeking political power, he is no threat to the Roman state. Even so, Pilate's mind has been poisoned by what he's heard. Just like Pilate, we often have distorted images of Jesus that come from many sources: religious authorities, the media, social structures, our own brokenness suffered at the hands of others. How can we allow Jesus to be the source of our truth and let him reform our understanding of who he is?

Continue the Conversation

Jesus: Is that your own idea or did others talk to you about me?

Me: Many people say you are the Messiah and have come to conquer. They really don't know who you are.

Wednesday, Week 5

· · · · · · · · · · · ·

Read Mark 10:35-45.

Then James and John, the sons of Zebedee, came to him. "Teacher," they said, "we want you to do for us whatever we ask." "What do you want me to do for you?" he asked. They replied, "Let one of us sit at your right and the other at your left in your glory." "You don't know what you are asking," Jesus said. **"Can you drink the cup I drink or be baptized with the baptism I am baptized with?"** "We can," they answered. Jesus said to them, "You will drink the cup I drink and be baptized with the baptism I am baptized with, but to sit at my right or left is not for me to grant. These places belong to those for whom they have been prepared." When the ten heard about this, they became indignant with James and John. Jesus called them together and said, "You know that those who are regarded as rulers of the Gentiles lord it over them, and their high officials exercise authority over them. Not so with you. Instead, whoever wants to become great among you must be your servant, and whoever wants to be first must be slave of all. For even the Son of Man did not come to be served, but to serve, and to give his life as a ransom for many."

Reflection

We have looked at this passage previously, focusing on Jesus' first question. This week, we return to consider Jesus' second question: "Can you drink the cup I drink or be baptized with the baptism I am baptized with?" James and John don't know what they are asking for when they request to be on Jesus' right and left in his glory. Knowing that Jesus will be crucified along with criminals on his right and left, we perhaps get a deeper sense of what it is that James and John have unknowingly asked for. After reading about what Jesus suffers in his trial, we understand all that is involved in sharing Jesus' sufferings: being betrayed by those closest to us, being misunderstood, being rejected by the powers that be. Drinking the cup that Jesus drank and being baptized in the same way Jesus was baptized—that is, suffering as Jesus has suffered—is only possible with Jesus' help. What of Jesus' sufferings is he inviting us to experience? Putting together Jesus' second question with his first, we might ask ourselves, *Does the path to the true desires of my heart lead through participating in Jesus' sufferings? What is it that I desire that will require dying with Christ?*

Continue the Conversation

Jesus: Can you drink the cup I drink or be baptized with the baptism I am baptized with?

Me: I cannot drink the cup you drink and be baptized with your baptism. You tell me me I will do more on Earth than you do. If we follow you we can grow in you and become more like you.

Thursday, Week 5

. . . .

Read John 13:1-10, 12-17.

It was just before the Passover Festival. Jesus knew that the hour had come for him to leave this world and go to the Father. Having loved his own who were in the world, he loved them to the end. The evening meal was in progress, and the devil had already prompted Judas, the son of Simon Iscariot, to betray Jesus. Jesus knew that the Father had put all things under his power, and that he had come from God and was returning to God; so he got up from the meal, took off his outer clothing, and wrapped a towel around his waist. After that, he poured water into a basin and began to wash his disciples' feet, drying them with the towel that was wrapped around him. He came to Simon Peter, who said to him, "Lord, are you going to wash my feet?" Jesus replied, "You do not realize now what I am doing, but later you will understand." "No," said Peter, "you shall never wash my feet." Jesus answered, "Unless I wash you, you have no part with me. "Then, Lord," Simon Peter replied, "not just my feet but my hands and my head as well!" Jesus answered, "Those who have had a bath need only to wash their feet; their whole body is clean. And you are clean . . ." . . . When he had finished washing their feet, he put on his clothes and returned to his place. **"Do you understand what I have done for you?"** he asked them. "You call me 'Teacher' and 'Lord,' and rightly so, for that is what I am. Now that I, your Lord and Teacher, have washed your feet, you also should wash one another's feet. I have set you an example that you should do as I have done for you. Very truly I tell you, no servant is greater than his master, nor is a messenger greater than the one who sent him. Now that you know these things, you will be blessed if you do them."

Reflection

In some ways, today's question is the one that the church has been trying to answer for almost two thousand years. In going to the cross, in suffering and dying for us and yet also at our hands, Jesus' death is an act of love (v. 1), humility (vv. 13-14), and service (v. 16). It is also an act that Jesus invites us to imitate (vv. 15, 17). What has Jesus done for us? How do we understand it?

Continue the Conversation

Jesus: Do you understand what I have done for you?

Me: ....

....

....

....

....

....

....

....

....

....

....

....

....

Friday, Week 5

· · · · · · · · · · · ·

Read Mark 15:22-37.

[The soldiers] brought Jesus to the place called Golgotha (which means "the place of the skull"). Then they offered him wine mixed with myrrh, but he did not take it. And they crucified him. Dividing up his clothes, they cast lots to see what each would get. It was nine in the morning when they crucified him. The written notice of the charge against him read: THE KING OF THE JEWS. They crucified two rebels with him, one on his right and one on his left. Those who passed by hurled insults at him, shaking their heads and saying, "So! You who are going to destroy the temple and build it in three days, come down from the cross and save yourself!" In the same way the chief priests and the teachers of the law mocked him among themselves. "He saved others," they said, "but he can't save himself! Let this Messiah, this king of Israel, come down now from the cross, that we may see and believe." Those crucified with him also heaped insults on him. At noon, darkness came over the whole land until three in the afternoon. And at three in the afternoon Jesus cried out in a loud voice, "*Eloi, Eloi, lema sabachthani*?" (which means "**My God, my God, why have you forsaken me?**"). When some of those standing near heard this, they said, "Listen, he's calling Elijah." Someone ran, filled a sponge with wine vinegar, put it on a staff, and offered it to Jesus to drink. "Now leave him alone. Let's see if Elijah comes to take him down," he said. With a loud cry, Jesus breathed his last.

Reflection

Convicted of treason, Jesus is condemned to die. His disciples have fled. Three times, Peter has denied knowing him. Passersby mock him, as do religious leaders. The sign above his head mocks his life's central message regarding the coming kingdom of God. Abandoned, misunderstood, mocked, and rejected, Jesus hangs on the cross, awaiting God's rescue. After all, he has taught that God is trustworthy to provide all that we need, that God is faithful to those who look to God—that laying down our life is the way to save it. Is it true? Mark's Gospel tells us that somehow this is Jesus' moment of glory. Yet Jesus cries out in honest desperation, "My God, my God, why have you forsaken me?" Even in this moment, Jesus turns to God through the words of his people. (See Psalm 22:1.) As we read about the crucifixion, we may have reason to cry out with him. Where in our lives are we waiting for God's rescue? Where do we feel abandoned? How is God's purpose for our lives difficult to see?

Continue the Conversation

Jesus: My God, my God, why have you forsaken me?

Me: (Repeat Jesus' words and then continue the conversation.) ....

....

....

....

....

....

....

....

....

....

....

....

....

....

Who Are You Looking For?

Though no one has ever accused me of being graceful, I spent the better part of a year taking ballroom dance lessons. It was my freshman year of college; my girlfriend suggested we take lessons, and I was in no position to refuse. I was a disaster on the dance floor. The instructors marveled that someone with a background in music could flail about with so little regard for the beat. I was mystified too. Standing without a musical instrument in my hands, I felt as though music had turned into an alien code. The notes seemed to come at random intervals. I was completely lost.

Week after week, my poor girlfriend suffered through my ineptitude. The instructors would regularly step in to rescue her from my incompetence, giving her a sense of what it would be like to dance with someone who knew what he was doing. From time to time, one of them would step in to dance with me, asking me to let him or her lead so I could get the feel of a step. And oftentimes it *worked*. Suddenly the steps and the beat of the music made sense together. The subtle push and pull of a good dancer and leader, someone who knew what he or she was doing, was enough to help me find my way.

• • • • • •

Early on what we now think of as the first Easter morning, Mary Magdalene, one of Jesus' dearest friends, is lost. Two days prior, Jesus, whom she had spent years following as he taught and healed people across the Judean countryside, was crucified. He was buried right before the start of the Jewish sabbath on Friday evening, so she hadn't been able to visit the tomb since that horrific night. So, as soon as she can, early Sunday morning, Mary goes to the tomb to prepare Jesus' body for burial, but she is met with a surprise:

> Early on the first day of the week, while it was still dark, Mary Magdalene came to the tomb and saw that the stone had been removed from the tomb. . . . Mary stood weeping outside the tomb. As she wept, she bent over to look into the tomb; and she saw two angels in white, sitting where the body of Jesus had been lying, one at the head and the other at the feet. They said to her, "Woman, why are you weeping?" She said to them, "They have taken away my Lord, and I do not know where they have laid him." (John 20:1, 11-13, NRSV)

Faced with the tragedy of Jesus' death, Mary does what she's done for the past few years. Even when his body is lying in a tomb, Mary follows Jesus. But, when she arrives at the tomb, Jesus' body is missing, so she doesn't know what to do.

> When [Mary] had said this, she turned around and saw Jesus standing there, but she did not know that it was Jesus. Jesus said to her, "Woman, why are you weeping? Whom are you looking for?" Supposing him to be the gardener, she said to him, "Sir, if you have carried him away, tell me where you have laid him, and I will take him away." Jesus said to her, "Mary!" She turned and said to him in Hebrew, "Rabbouni!" (which means Teacher). (John 20:14-16, NRSV)

Mary is the first to see Jesus resurrected. At Jesus' urging, she runs and tells his other disciples. The good news of Easter—that Jesus, whom we killed, nevertheless lives!—begins to spread. The question Jesus asks her is simply this: "Who are you looking for?" If all we had was this story, the question wouldn't be all that remarkable. But this question is a significant one in the Gospel of John. In Greek, it's almost exactly the same question Jesus asks his first disciples in John 1: "What are you looking for?" (v. 38). In that context, it's clear that both Jesus' question and the disciples' answer are operating on more than one level. Jesus is asking them what they're seeking, what they're after, what they're about in life.

This is the fundamental question of the Gospel of John: What are you seeking? Some seek their own glory. (See John 5:44; 7:18; 8:50.) Some seek Jesus because of what he can do for them. (See John 6:24.) Pilate seeks a way out of condemning an innocent man. (See John 19:12.) Jesus seeks to do the will of his heavenly Father. (See John 5:30.) Many seek to have Jesus arrested and killed. (See John 5:18; 7:1, 19-20, 25, 30; 8:37, 40; 10:39; 11:8; 18:4, 7-8.)

What we seek reveals who we are. We're intentional beings; just about everything we do is for some purpose, for the sake of something we're seeking. Day in and day out, we chase after all kinds of things. Some of those things—like money, sex, power, success, and self—can leave us dissatisfied even when we get what we want. Other things are more substantial: justice, beauty, home, identity, meaning, relationship, purpose. Jesus wants to know who we are and what we value. He isn't asking, "What are your politics?", "What are your ethics?", or even "What is your religion?" Certainly, how we live and what we believe are important, but Jesus concerns himself with where the arrow of our life is pointing. Who or what we're seeking—where we're pointed—determines so much more than where we happen to be at the moment. This is important for us to know because we may sense that Jesus' first question is about where we are, and that question may tell us that we are disqualified from life with Jesus. Instead, we find Jesus asking us this question: "What are you looking for?" This question is not about our location but instead about the direction of our lives. This sort of question makes room for us in a different way, turns disqualification into an invitation to transformation. As it turns out, when it comes to that deeper constellation of longings, Jesus regularly meets us in these pursuits—whether or not we know from the outset that Jesus can be found in these things.

In my own life, my big pursuit has been for truth—whether as a student, a teacher, or a scholar. Also, as an INTJ on the Myers-Briggs Type Indicator, I am inclined almost pathologically toward certainty. I need to know the truth, and I need to be certain. I can honestly say that the revolution that Jesus has brought about in my life over the last twenty years has had everything to do with revealing himself as the Truth. Especially during my time in seminary, when, as I described in the last chapter, my certainties about life, the world, and what I thought I knew about God started to shift, I found that only Jesus was sufficient as a foundation. Not stories or ideas *about* Jesus. Those could be—and often were—cold, dead, unfeeling. No, I came to find that while I had started out after truth in the generic sense, what I was really after—whether I knew it or not—was the Truth who is a person: Jesus.

This is why the arc of the Gospel of John takes us from "What are you looking for?" to "Who are you looking for?" Because, in the end, what we're really looking for—what we really need—is not an abstraction or an idea. We're not looking for a *what*; we're looking for a *who*. Jesus is the one we seek. When we dig deep, when we keep pressing, we find that what's real, what's at the heart of what we're after is Jesus. His embrace—too near to leave us less than transformed. His love—too deep to leave us as we are. His provision—too abundant for words. His presence—a power that creates life out of death. That can sound like pious talk—this idea that Jesus and only Jesus has what we really want and that somehow Jesus knows better than we do about our heart's desire. But that's the core of the invitation that Jesus has for us: the promise that Jesus has what we're looking for, what's *worth* seeking. Moreover, he himself is what's worth pursuing.

Suppose we're driving late at night in an unfamiliar place, and we're a bit turned around, trying to find our way back to the highway. (For this metaphor, we have to imagine that we're living in a pre-GPS world.) It's foggy, and we can hardly see the road in front of us. Just as we consider pulling off to the shoulder, we see a set of taillights in front of us. This driver seems to know where he's going. He takes the corners confidently—even amid the fog. Perhaps the driver knows this road. Following this car at least keeps us from swerving off the pavement and, for the moment, with whatever vague sense we have of which way the highway is, we start to get the sense that this driver is also headed the same direction. So, when we reach an intersection and are unsure how to proceed, we take a leap of faith and follow the car ahead. Sure enough, we see a sign that suggests we're going the right way. Slowly, our confidence builds. After a couple more intersections, we decide to keep following those taillights in front of us, with a growing sense that they will keep us on the road and get us where we're trying to go.

This story illustrates the transition from seeking various good things we want to seeking Jesus. First, we notice that Jesus seems to know something about how to keep life on track, how to stay on the road. Then, we sense that Jesus is going where we wish our lives were headed, but we don't know the best way. Maybe Jesus affirms a couple of our hunches about life: the centrality of relationship, the importance of justice, our responsibility to the poor, the preciousness of beauty, the value of meaning and purpose, the elusive significance of truth. Before long, we start to get a sense that Jesus is headed where we've wanted to go all along, and we start to follow him, trusting that he knows the best way to get there. To be sure, Jesus takes some puzzling turns along the way — moments where our nascent trust is put to the test. We may find ourselves answering even more questions: Will I find my purpose in life by laying it down for others? Does justice require me to take the short end of the stick? But, over time, our hunch becomes conviction, and bit by bit we're willing to follow Jesus' counterintuitive turns along the road.

Eventually, the path along the road with Jesus — the journey itself — becomes valuable to us. Like Mary, we get to the point where we have no doubt; the arrow of our life points toward Jesus. He is where we're headed. Jesus now has the authority to change the destination itself, to shape what we recognize as just, what we mean by greatness, what we know to be beautiful, what the criteria are for truth. It's here that the metaphor begins to shift. Now, the experience is like learning to dance with a gifted instructor. The push, the pull, the subtle cues lead us where we need to go, helping us become what we could not be on our own. At first, each step we take feels like a tremendous risk, like a leap into the unknown.

But there is no other way to do it; the dance has begun, and we must learn as we go. Sometimes we take steps and find that we meet our partner exactly where expected. Other times, our partner's wry smile greets us, and we realize we ought to have gone the other way. Occasionally, we step on a toe, and our partner's face has a pained grimace to go with that wry smile. But our partner is so gifted that even our missteps get incorporated into the dance. There is leadership here, no doubt, but also partnership. From time to time, our partner gives us a look that tells us the next move is our choice; we are invited to share in the joy of improvising this dance, making moves appropriate to the moment, feeling the rhythm of the dance itself.

Once we enter wholeheartedly into this dance, our pursuit of justice always and everywhere has to do with our pursuit of the One—Jesus—who proclaims the dawn of transformative justice while suffering at the hands of our injustice. Our pursuit of beauty always and everywhere has to do with our pursuit of the One who founded beauty itself and who reveals in his life a beauty no less basic and profound than life out of death. Our pursuit of truth always and everywhere becomes a pursuit of the One who declares himself to be the Truth. Following Jesus changes everything.

• • • • • •

But, of course, all this Mary already knows. This is already the orientation of her life. The arrow of her life points to Jesus. Right from the start, we see Mary doing what she knows to do: seeking Jesus. Yet, she's at a loss at the empty tomb. Where is she supposed to go if Jesus cannot be found? We can hear the despair in her voice: "They have taken away my Lord, and I don't know where they have laid him." She's stuck but, thankfully, mistaken. No one has taken Jesus anywhere. She doesn't understand what's going on and can't begin to imagine that Jesus is risen from the dead. So she's seeking—but she's seeking a dead man.

Then, Jesus speaks her name: "Mary."

The fact that Jesus is alive makes all the difference because it means that the One Mary is seeking is also seeking her. This is the good news of the Resurrection:

The One we're looking for is also looking for us. And our enmity, our apathy, our impotence—even death itself—cannot hold him back. Jesus seeks Mary after everything that befell him—after Judas betrayed him, the crowd demanded his execution, his disciples scattered. The women who followed him, like Mary, were powerless to stop his death; nevertheless, Jesus seeks those who seek him. He pursues Mary in love, speaking her name.

Seeking on its own will only get us so far. Because seeking is something we do, it can have limitations. Like Mary, when it comes down to our seeking, we're at the mercy of others—what they've done with Jesus, where they've put him, what they've made of him. A corpse, after all, is posed according to the desires of those who maintain the body. We see this in our world in the many "Jesuses" put forward and maintained by various stakeholders, be they preachers or politicians. We went through a litany of them in the previous chapter. It's enough to make us dizzy—or give up on our search altogether.

Perhaps we have found ourselves chasing after Jesus as though we're looking for a *dead* man—a great teacher of long ago, a hero, an idea, a principle, a relic of a religion. Inevitably, we hit snags along the way in the form of questions we can't answer and doubts we can't shake. We may have asked ourselves if our search is futile. And it would be if we're simply playing *Weekend at Bernie's* with Jesus' legacy, using a dead man's body as a puppet for our own purposes. But a corpse makes for a terrible dance partner—much less, a *lead* partner. Unless Jesus is an active agent in the world, unless Jesus is alive—unless the One we seek is seeking us—then everything about seeking beauty in Jesus rather than beauty itself, seeking justice in Jesus, and seeking truth in Jesus is just pure semantics, a pious way of continuing life as it already was. But if Jesus *is* alive, if the One we seek is seeking us, then we have nothing less than what the Bible calls the *gospel*: the good news that everything we've been chasing, everything we've ever wanted, everything we need for abundant life is found in a *person* and that person is alive and at work in the world. He's seeking us, engaging us, and pursuing us. He's there, hidden in plain sight, whispering our name. He conquered the grave to be with us.

• • • • • •

As long as I've known her, my wife, Hannah, has committed herself to the work of justice. She's intrinsically drawn to the margins, whether that's at a party or at the societal level. Hannah naturally seeks people who need someone to help them connect; she sees people's needs. She's drawn to the poor and is constantly asking questions, such as, "Why is this person on the margins? What can be done?" She moves quickly from the individual to the system. Her passion for people quickly turns to seeking justice for her neighbors. It's no surprise that her pursuit of Jesus has always been joined with Jesus' pursuit of justice. On the other hand, as I mentioned earlier, much of my life has been oriented around the pursuit of truth, which has led me down the path of becoming a teacher and a scholar. And, as I said, along that path, I've encountered Jesus in some pretty profound ways.

Hannah's vocation and my vocation haven't always worked together well. Scholarship tends to be an elite pursuit—at times an *elitist* pursuit. It can feel like the polar opposite of Hannah's passion. Early in our marriage, we struggled with how to make major life decisions, straddling these two sets of priorities. Our vocations even diverged geographically: I felt like academic work required me to be in the United States; Hannah felt like her pursuit of justice meant being with the poorest of the poor at the farthest reaches of the globe. We began asking ourselves, *Is this relationship tenable? Does commitment to this relationship mean that one of us will have to be disobedient to what God has called us to pursue?*

Amid these tensions, many years ago, Hannah and I attended a regional leadership conference for the Vineyard movement—the community of churches to which our church belongs. I'll never forget what happened. The national director of the Vineyard was speaking and, as he was wrapping up, he said he felt that God wanted us to pray for folks in the room who were under thirty. He went on to say that he felt like God especially was highlighting two groups of folks that God had particular callings upon, two groups of folks who embodied the synthesis of what God was calling us into as a community of churches. God, he said, wanted to encourage both those called to social justice and those called to a life of scholarship. Hannah and I fit these categories perfectly: We were under thirty, with one of us called to social justice and the other to academia. He may as well have said, "Everyone, let's gather around to pray; God wants to encourage Hannah and Matt." We were amazed with the sense that our vocations were reconcilable, and we felt confident that our desires for what we sought were placed in our hearts by God.

More than anything, what we took from that night was simply this: We were known. In that invitation to prayer, Jesus spoke our names. We knew that Jesus was alive, that God was real, and that the One we were seeking was seeking us. That's always how it goes. What changes our lives when we hear from God is not so much *what* we hear as the fact *that* we hear. It's not so much what God says as the fact that God speaks, that God sees us and knows us. Jesus wants to know who we're looking for, but, even more than that, he wants us to know that he's looking for us.

Monday, Week 6

· · · · · · · · · · · ·

Read John 20:1, 11-18, NRSV.

Early on the first day of the week, while it was still dark, Mary Magdalene came to the tomb and saw that the stone had been removed from the tomb. . . . Mary stood weeping outside the tomb. As she wept, she bent over to look into the tomb; and she saw two angels in white, sitting where the body of Jesus had been lying, one at the head and the other at the feet. They said to her, "Woman, why are you weeping?" She said to them, "They have taken away my Lord, and I do not know where they have laid him." When she had said this, she turned around and saw Jesus standing there, but she did not know that it was Jesus. Jesus said to her, "Woman, why are you weeping? **Whom are you looking for?**" Supposing him to be the gardener, she said to him, "Sir, if you have carried him away, tell me where you have laid him, and I will take him away." Jesus said to her, "Mary!" She turned and said to him in Hebrew, "Rabbouni!" (which means Teacher). Jesus said to her, "Do not hold on to me, because I have not yet ascended to the Father. But go to my brothers and say to them, 'I am ascending to my Father and your Father, to my God and your God.'" Mary Magdalene went and announced to the disciples, "I have seen the Lord"; and she told them that he had said these things to her.

Reflection

Mary's world has been turned upside down. Jesus has died. What can she do; where can she go? She decides to go to Jesus' tomb to be with him. There, Jesus appears to her, though she doesn't recognize him. Jesus asks her, "Why are you weeping? Whom are you looking for?" The second question is almost exactly the same as the question Jesus asks his disciples in John 1:38: "What are you looking for?" The question is still about seeking. Mary Magdalene is searching for Jesus. She cries because she doesn't know what to do or where to go without him. Then Jesus speaks her name. And she recognizes him. "Rabbouni!" she exclaims. He is her teacher, the one whom she follows, whom she seeks. Our question for today is this: Who or what are we seeking? What would bring us sorrow if it were lost? Our answer may not be (at least not exclusively) *Jesus*. If so, we can be honest with Jesus about that. When we listen for Jesus to speak our name, no matter how often we get confused or distracted, we know that he is always and everywhere seeking us.

Continue the Conversation

Jesus: Whom are you looking for?

Me: *I am looking for the one who is going to save the world. You came to forgive my sins and make me righteous in front of God.*

Tuesday, Week 6

· · · · · · · · · · · ·

Read Luke 24:36-49.

While [the disciples] were still talking about this, Jesus himself stood among them and said to them, "Peace be with you." They were startled and frightened, thinking they saw a ghost. He said to them, "**Why are you troubled, and why do doubts rise in your minds?** Look at my hands and my feet. It is I myself! Touch me and see; a ghost does not have flesh and bones, as you see I have." When he had said this, he showed them his hands and feet. And while they still did not believe it because of joy and amazement, he asked them, "Do you have anything here to eat?" They gave him a piece of broiled fish, and he took it and ate it in their presence. He said to them, "This is what I told you while I was still with you: Everything must be fulfilled that is written about me in the Law of Moses, the Prophets and the Psalms." Then he opened their minds so they could understand the Scriptures. He told them, "This is what is written: The Messiah will suffer and rise from the dead on the third day, and repentance for the forgiveness of sins will be preached in his name to all nations, beginning at Jerusalem. You are witnesses of these things. I am going to send you what my Father has promised; but stay in the city until you have been clothed with power from on high."

Reflection

The disciples are faced with a reality that seems too good to be true: Their crucified Lord is standing before them, alive. Jesus shows himself to them, inviting them to come, touch, and see, so they will believe he is who he says he is. Through God's miraculous intervention, Jesus has conquered death itself. Almost two thousand years later, this story still may seem too good—or too strange—to be true. Death itself has been conquered; Jesus' upside-down way of life has been vindicated. Apparently, laying down our lives really is the way to save them. The disciples had doubts, and so do we. Jesus' question is relevant to us today, and he is willing to engage in our doubts. He invites us to experience the reality of his resurrection through prayer, scripture, worship, and the community his presence builds.

Continue the Conversation

Jesus: Why are you troubled, and why do doubts rise in your minds?

Me: _The doubts come when I lose your strength in me. My flesh is so weak_

Wednesday, Week 6

· · · · · · · · · · · ·

Read John 21:1-9, 15-17.

Jesus appeared again to his disciples, by the Sea of Galilee. It happened this way: Simon Peter, Thomas (also known as Didymus), Nathanael from Cana in Galilee, the sons of Zebedee, and two other disciples were together. "I'm going out to fish," Simon Peter told them, and they said, "We'll go with you." So they went out and got into the boat, but that night they caught nothing. Early in the morning, Jesus stood on the shore, but the disciples did not realize that it was Jesus. He called out to them, "Friends, haven't you any fish?" "No," they answered. He said, "Throw your net on the right side of the boat and you will find some." When they did, they were unable to haul the net in because of the large number of fish. Then the disciple whom Jesus loved said to Peter, "It is the Lord!" As soon as Simon Peter heard him say, "It is the Lord," he wrapped his outer garment around him (for he had taken it off) and jumped into the water. The other disciples followed in the boat, towing the net full of fish, for they were not far from shore, about a hundred yards. When they landed, they saw a fire of burning coals there with fish on it, and some bread. . . . When they had finished eating, Jesus said to Simon Peter, "Simon son of John, **do you love me more than these?**" "Yes, Lord," he said, "you know that I love you." Jesus said, "Feed my lambs." Again Jesus said, "Simon son of John, do you love me?" He answered, "Yes, Lord, you know that I love you." Jesus said, "Take care of my sheep." The third time he said to him, "Simon son of John, do you love me?" Peter was hurt because Jesus asked him the third time, "Do you love me?" He said, "Lord, you know all things; you know that I love you." Jesus said, "Feed my sheep."

Reflection

Unsure of where to go or what to do after Jesus' death, Peter returns to the life he knows: fishing. But Jesus has bigger plans for him. He asks Peter about his priorities: "Do you love me more than these?"—that is, more than you love your boat, your nets, and so on. This is no small question. Fishing was Peter's life before he began following Jesus; it was his identity. Nevertheless, Peter says yes. As a result, Jesus invites Peter to feed and take care of Jesus' sheep, that is, to pastor and shepherd the community Jesus is building. Jesus also wants to know if we love him more than the things of life. Do we love Jesus more than our work? more than our studies? more than the identities we had before we began following him? If so, Jesus invites us to invest deeply in the lives of the people around us.

Continue the Conversation

Jesus: Do you love me more than these?

Me: yes, I love you Lord. Help me to grow in your love and give more, love more, share more,

Thursday, Week 6

. . . .

Read John 21:17-23.

Jesus said, "Feed my sheep. Very truly I tell you, when you were younger you dressed yourself and went where you wanted; but when you are old you will stretch out your hands, and someone else will dress you and lead you where you do not want to go." Jesus said this to indicate the kind of death by which Peter would glorify God. Then he said to him, "Follow me!" Peter turned and saw that the disciple whom Jesus loved was following them. (This was the one who had leaned back against Jesus at the supper and had said, "Lord, who is going to betray you?") When Peter saw him, he asked, "Lord, what about him?" Jesus answered, **"If I want him to remain alive until I return, what is that to you?** You must follow me." Because of this, the rumor spread among the believers that this disciple would not die. But Jesus did not say that he would not die; he only said, "If I want him to remain alive until I return, what is that to you?"

Reflection

After all that Peter has been through—declaring his devotion to Jesus, denying him three times, seeing Jesus resurrected—Jesus' call remains the same: "Follow me!" This time, however, Jesus offers more precise information about the cost of obedience. Peter—like Jesus—will glorify God through his death. Rather than protest (like he did when Jesus first told him about Jesus' own coming death) or run away (like he did at Jesus' trial), Peter simply wants to know that the cost of discipleship is fair. We get the sense that Peter points to the disciple nearest him to find out if he's getting a raw deal: "What about him?" Jesus' answer is in the form of a question: "If I want him to remain alive until I return, what is that to you?"

The cost of following Jesus is universal (always costly) but by no means uniform (not everyone incurs the same costs). We easily can get caught up in comparing our life following Jesus with others', envying someone else's "easier" path or judging someone else for not walking the same path Jesus asks us to walk. But Jesus wants to know if we are willing to stop comparing our paths to others' paths and simply follow him.

Continue the Conversation

Jesus: [If I give someone else an "easier" path to follow], what is that to you?

Me: ....

....

....

....

....

....

....

....

....

....

....

....

....

Friday, Week 6

· · · · · · · · · · · ·

Read John 11:1, 3, 17, 20-27, 32-44.

A man named Lazarus was sick. He was from Bethany, the village of Mary and her sister Martha. . . . So the sisters sent word to Jesus, "Lord, the one you love is sick." . . . On his arrival, Jesus found that Lazarus had already been in the tomb for four days. . . . When Martha heard that Jesus was coming, she went out to meet him, but Mary stayed at home. "Lord," Martha said to Jesus, "if you had been here, my brother would not have died. But I know that even now God will give you whatever you ask." Jesus said to her, "Your brother will rise again." Martha answered, "I know he will rise again in the resurrection at the last day." Jesus said to her, "I am the resurrection and the life. The one who believes in me will live, even though they die; and whoever lives by believing in me will never die. **Do you believe this?**" "Yes, Lord," she replied, "I believe that you are the Messiah, the Son of God, who is to come into the world." . . . When Mary reached the place where Jesus was and saw him, she fell at his feet and said, "Lord, if you had been here, my brother would not have died." When Jesus saw her weeping, and the Jews who had come along with her also weeping, he was deeply moved in spirit and troubled. "Where have you laid him?" he asked. "Come and see, Lord," they replied. Jesus wept. Then the Jews said, "See how he loved him!" But some of them said, "Could not he who opened the eyes of the blind man have kept this man from dying?" Jesus, once more deeply moved, came to the tomb. It was a cave with a stone laid across the entrance. "Take away the stone," he said. "But, Lord," said Martha, the sister of the dead man, "by this time there is a bad odor, for he has been there four days." Then Jesus said, "**Did I not tell you that if you believe, you will see the glory of God?**" So they took away the stone. Then Jesus looked up and said, "Father, I thank you that you have heard me. I knew that you always hear me, but I said this for the benefit of the people standing here, that they may believe that you sent me." When he had said this, Jesus called in a loud voice, "Lazarus, come out!" The dead man came out, his hands and feet wrapped with strips of linen, and a cloth around his face. Jesus said to them, "Take off the grave clothes and let him go."

Reflection

Martha's theology is impeccable. When Jesus tells her that her brother will be raised from the dead, she responds that she understands he will be raised at the resurrection—that is, at the end of the world when God's kingdom is fully realized. Jesus insists that the resurrection is not a future event; it's a person. Jesus himself is the resurrection. Jesus asks, "Did I not tell you that if you believe, you will see the glory of God?"—not just in the hereafter but in the here and now. Jesus acts upon the truth of what he says by calling out to the dead man, and the dead man walks out of his grave.

Jesus has a similar question for us: "Do you believe that life is found in me?" As we've taken the risk to speak honestly with Jesus about the desires of our heart, what have we seen God do? What are we still waiting to see? Jesus' promise also contains a paradox: "The one who believes in me will live, even though they die." As we've seen throughout our time in scripture, following Jesus in no way shields us from the pain of life. Indeed, Jesus himself weeps with Mary and Martha as they mourn their brother's death. Nevertheless, following Jesus means that we live with hope that God intervenes in our world with resurrection power. Let us thank Jesus for what we've seen him do and ask for the endurance to wait in hope for what still lies ahead.

Continue the Conversation

Jesus: I am the resurrection and the life. The one who believes in me will live, even though they die; and whoever lives by believing in me will never die. Do you believe this? Did I not tell you that if you believe, you will see the glory of God?

Me: I believe in the resurrection and the life. I believe I will never die. I believe I will see the glory of God.

EPILOGUE

You began this journey with an invitation to engage in conversation with Jesus—even if only as an experiment. If you made it this far, I'll assume that you've stumbled across *something* that gave you the sense that there's someone else on the other end of the line. So where can you go from here?

In my experience, the key is to *continue the conversation*. Jesus asks more questions in the Gospels than those listed in this book—over 250 more. If you've finished the exercises in this book, you may consider responding to some of Jesus' other questions. Or dialogue with Jesus through the Psalms or through the Daily Office from The Book of Common Prayer. In a certain sense, it doesn't matter *what* you say in your conversation with Jesus. When it comes to the spiritual life, who you talk to is more important than what you say. Your questions aren't as important as the person to whom you address your questions. Even if you use the Psalms as the words of your prayers, thinking that somehow these (or any other words) are the "right" words to pray would be foolish. Instead, the Psalms demonstrate that *any words*—even despondent, angry, or violent words—can be constructive if and when addressed to God. (Seriously, if you haven't read the Psalms, take a look; they contain a full range of human emotion. Some of them are downright shocking.) As disappointed, frustrated, or lost as you may feel from time to time, dare to address your disappointment, frustration, and anguish in prayer to God rather than letting a sense of propriety or shame sucker you into letting the conversation lapse—either by putting on airs of piety or cutting off communication entirely. Candor with God is key.

As you continue to speak honestly with Jesus, you also continue to listen. Prayer—and that, after all, is what you've been doing these past six weeks—is a dialogue, not a monologue. The goal is not simply to vent but to invite Jesus to respond, to gain his perspective, and to enter into a closer relationship with him. Sometimes, you may need to come to Jesus in silence. Even when you have no words, you can listen. In speech and in silence, incline your ears to hear the voice of the One who is always and everywhere pursuing you in love.